for Sus k

Sue this is a fantastic cookbook! It is easy   ow and easy to read. So much information, even for someone not incorporating the HGC into their daily plan...and so many people should be. I am confident this book will increase your business 100 fold!

- Suzanne Gravelle, Halifax, Nova Scotia
Author of 'Unfinished'

You have a fine selection of ingredients to use – some which are simple (like the one with a jar of salsa and chicken – my husband loved that one) and some that have a few more ingredients. In either case, these are quick, simple and tasty dishes, and I had no trouble putting them together from scratch. I get home around 5:15, and with your recipes, I have dinner ready to eat usually no later than 6:00pm.

- Diana Berry, Lethbridge, Alberta

The recipes in your cookbook made it so much easier for me and my husband to stick to the HCG Diet. We sometimes forgot we were on a restricted diet! It's amazing how you've managed to create recipes for yummy dishes and meals from such a limited ingredient list. We can't wait for your Phase 3 cookbook!

Suzette and John Drake, British Columbia

I like to cook, but it was difficult to make interesting meals with the limited allowable foods and ingredients on the HCG Diet. So, I went online and bought every HCG cookbook I could find. Sue, I can honestly say that yours is the best.

- Monica, Alberta

Published in Canada by Susan Lillemo, hcgrecipesbook.com, hcgmetamorphosis.com

First Edition published April, 2012

Cover art and design by DesJardins NuMedia
Cover content and internal design © 2012 by Susan Lillemo

Published by Susan Lillemo with the assistance of DesJardins NuMedia

ISBN-13: 978-0988010000 (Susan Lillemo)
ISBN-10: 0988010003

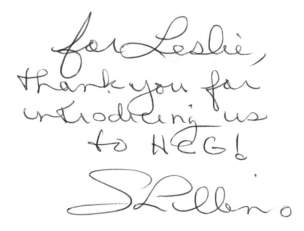

for Leslie,
thank you for
introducing us
to HCG!
S. Lillemo

DEDICATION

I dedicate this book to my husband, Al. Over the past thirty years he has encouraged me to learn… and to grow… and to do. I have grown so much because of you, Al. Thank you for your support and love.

And, a very special thanks to Dave, my son and business partner. Without him, this book would not have happened. Thank you, Dave, for all you are and all you do.

~ Susan Lillemo

TABLE OF CONTENTS

INTRODUCTION

First of all, thank you for purchasing this book! I am confident that you will find value in your purchase, not only for ideas on how to prepare such a limited list of ingredients, but also for the cooking and health tips I have included.

Having positively affected so many lives by distributing the HCG product, and giving people a chance to truly enjoy who they are, I have had many requests for ideas and recipes over that period of time. This has inspired me to create this book for you!

Congratulations for taking control of your health by taking this important step to regain a healthy weight. There are numerous health issues that develop as a result of excess weight, and many medications are prescribed in an attempt to control the symptoms that subsequently appear.

It is my belief that the first line of defense to ensure good health is understanding how to make good food choices, second is supplementation, and lastly, and certainly the least desirable, is the use of doctor prescribed medications. It is an unknown fact to most people that prescription medications are statistically the third leading cause of death in North America.

Therefore, I have also included nutritional information on the value of certain foods. Use this information to educate yourself on how to improve your health by simply making healthier food choices in your daily living.

Spices and herbs are important for adding flavor and interest to many dishes, so I have outlined the nutritional benefits of these herbs and spices, and hope that you continue to reap their benefits by incorporating them into your permanent lifestyle.

Included in this book are bonus reports on:
1) An explanation of the different phases of the HCG Diet protocol
2) Buying organic vs non-organic
3) The importance of hormone balance
4) A short Glycemic Index of common foods; a reference you can use for Phase Three of the HCG Diet protocol.

The larger print size I've chosen for this book will make it easier to reference while in the kitchen preparing your meals. Being visually challenged myself, I would expect this feature to benefit at least a few of you.

When you have completed Phase Two, the 500-calorie phase of the HCG Diet protocol, you may continue to use these recipes. Simply adjust them for Phase Three, which allows you to add a wider variety of fruits and vegetables, and wherein portion size and fats are not restricted.

I hope you will enjoy these recipes! You can make them a permanent part of your life.

Stay tuned for my next cookbook dedicated to Phase Three!

Why The Butterfly?

At this time, I would like to explain the butterfly logo on my book cover. First, I love butterflies. I love their beauty and their grace but even more, I love the process of how a caterpillar hides out in a cocoon, and will later emerge as a totally different creature – a beautiful butterfly! A caterpillar is restricted from moving freely and reaching heights because of its body – but after the metamorphosis, he is a new creature, free to fly and be admired. I encourage you to emerge from your cocoon.

I wish you a Metamorphosis!!

I welcome your contact. If you have any comments on this book or questions while on the HCG Diet, you may email me at: *support@hcgrecipesbook.com*

Connect with me also on Facebook:
http://www.facebook.com/hcgrecipesbook

Here's to you… a thinner and healthier YOU!

~ Susan Lillemo

THE PHASES OF THE HCG PROTOCOL

PHASE ONE
Two days in duration

*The first two days of taking the HCG drops
are the gorging days.*

Take 10 to 15 drops under the tongue, three times per day, and eat whatever you like... and plenty of it. Stuff yourself. The reason for this is to replenish all natural fat stores.

Natural fat stores are chronically deficient in people that are always "watching what they eat" or in those who are chronic yo-yo dieters.

This normal fat pads our organs, our faces, our joints and the pads of our feet, and it needs to be replenished.

You will most likely gain weight, but don't worry; it will be gone in just a couple of days. Some people actually lose weight while gorging; either way, it is okay.

If you gorge mostly on processed foods, junk food or foods high in sugar, you may suffer a headache on day 3 or 4. You can take a pain reliever for this. Once the headache is over, it won't return.

Enjoy yourself! This stage will help you keep on track while on the diet. The ones that don't gorge find they don't feel as well in the first week as the ones that do gorge.

PHASE TWO
Duration is 21 days minimum
or until you reach your goal

To begin Phase Two, on Day 3 of the HCG protocol, you drop your food intake to 500 calories.

Continue to take your drops three times per day. 10 to 15 drops are recommended but if you feel hunger, you may take more drops. You can even take an extra dose if you need to, it won't hurt you.

You must stick closely to the diet outlined. No substitutions! Weigh your meat raw before cooking. Read labels to be sure there is no sugar hiding out in spices, herb blends and seasonings. This diet has not only been calculated for caloric intake, but also for chemical balance.

Some may think, "I can have cabbage so why not Brussels sprouts?" or "If I can have chicken breast, why not turkey breast?" or "Green peppers are low in calories and low in carbohydrate, so why not add them into the diet?" Dr. Simeons was well aware of these food choices and, for whatever reason, due to his research, chose not to put them on the list.

If the food is not on the diet plan, don't eat it.

".... if a patient drops the apple and eats an extra Melba instead, he will not be getting more calories but he will not lose weight.

There are a number of foods, particularly fruits and vegetables, which have the same or even lower caloric

---

values than those listed as permissible, and yet we find that they interfere with the regular loss of weight under HCG, presumably owing to the nature of their composition."

- Page 22 of 'Pounds and Inches' by Dr. Simeons

THE HCG DIET PLAN

The 500-calorie diet is started on your Third day of drops.

Tea or coffee is allowed in any quantity – do not use sugar. Only 1 Tablespoon of milk is allowed in 24 hours. Stevia may be used. Green, Yerba Matte, Oolong and Chamomile teas are preferred.

BREAKFAST: no breakfast, however, you may eat the allowed foods in the allowed amounts any time of day. For example you might have an apple for breakfast.

LUNCH:
1. 100 GRAMS OF VEAL, BEEF, VENISON, BUFFALO, CHICKEN BREAST, FRESH WHITE FISH, LOBSTER, CRAB OR SHRIMP. All visible fat must be carefully removed before cooking and the meat must be weighed raw. It must be boiled or grilled without additional fat. Salmon, eel, tuna, herring, dried or pickled fish are not allowed. The chicken breast must be removed from the bird before cooking to avoid fat.

2. One choice of vegetable to be chosen from the following: spinach, chard, chicory, beet greens, green salad, tomatoes, celery, fennel, onions, red radishes, cucumbers, asparagus or cabbage. Amount is not limited. **You may make a salad with the allowed vegetables.**

3. One breadstick (grissini) or one Melba toast.

4. An apple or a handful of strawberries or ½ grapefruit or an orange.

DINNER:
You have the same four choices as for lunch. For best results, eat a different protein source than what you ate for lunch.

OTHER:
The juice of one lemon is allowed for all purposes. Salt, pepper, vinegar, mustard powder, garlic, basil, parsley, thyme, marjoram, etc. may be used for seasoning, but no oil, butter or dressing.

Tea, coffee, plain water or mineral water are the only drinks allowed, but are allowed in any quantity. Avoid peppermint tea. Green Tea is an excellent choice.

Drink a minimum of two litres of water per day. Your body will be more likely to store water if you don't drink enough. Water is also needed to wash away toxins and fat.

No lotions or cosmetics that contain oil are permitted, but mineral powders may be used. All products used must be oil free. Shampoo & conditioner are allowed, but keep the conditioner away from the scalp. No mouthwash or gum. Baking soda may be used for brushing teeth, if desired, or natural toothpaste.

No variations of this may be introduced. All things not listed are forbidden.

REQUIRED SUPPLEMENTS:

Take 1000 mcg of vitamin B12 each day – this is good for energy and well-being.

If you find your energy lagging in the afternoon, you may take a second dose.

Do not take this close to bedtime; it works so well for energy that it may disrupt your sleep.

Take 100 mg of Potassium per day. This helps keep your electrolytes and water table balanced. If you experience night leg cramps, take a second dose.

OPTIONS & VARIATIONS

The HCG Drops Vary Greatly
From The Live Hormone Injections

Immunity is not a problem with the drops, so, if you wish, you may stay on Phase Two until you reach your goal weight. If you need to take a break for a week or two, you may go to the maintenance phase, and then go back on the diet to reach your goal. There is no required 6-week break between Phases if you want to carry on. There is no need to gorge again – just eat normally the first two days you go back on the drops, and then drop to the 500 calories on the third day.

Dr. Simeons recommends that no medications be taken while on the HCG; understand that although that applies to the injection formula, it does not apply while taking the HCG diet drops. **Take your medications as usual** and as your weight comes down, you may find that you no longer need them. Cortisone, antidepressants and diuretics can slow your weight loss progress.

If a person develops an aversion to meat, eggs may be substituted on occasion. Due to the high fat content in the egg yolk, you are allowed one egg mixed with three egg whites as a substitute for meat or fish.

Another substitution is skimmed milk cottage cheese; you may have 100 grams occasionally, instead of the meat or fish, but no other cheeses are allowed.

Vegetarianism presents a special problem, as milk and curds are the only animal protein they can eat. To get enough protein of animal origin they must drink two cups (500 mL) of skim milk for dinner and again for supper. 100 grams of cottage cheese is another alternative.

The usual intake of vegetable protein from beans, wheat, nuts, etc., are not allowed. The average loss is about half that of non-vegetarians, perhaps due to the sugar content of the milk. Another option may be a protein/meal replacement shake. This option is not outlined by Dr. Simeons; however, I have personally tested one brand that has been a successful addition to the Phase Two protocol, however I cannot recommend any others, as I have not tested them. The protein must be high and the carbohydrates very low, and preferably of excellent quality - organic and non-GMO. Whey protein is the best.

It is recommended that you stop **supplementation of vitamins** while on the HCG protocol. Certainly, any oil-based supplements are not allowed. The jury is out as to whether or not the supplements interfere with the delicate chemical interactions taking place while on the HCG Diet.

To err on the safe side, I would recommend that you stop supplementation while on the protocol, if that would be reasonable for you.

Every time you lose a pound of fatty tissue, only the actual fat is burned up. All the vitamins, the proteins, the blood and the minerals, which this tissue contained in abundance, are fed back into the body. Even a low iron blood count can improve during treatment.

Dr. Simeons never encountered a significant protein deficiency or signs of a lack of vitamins in patients who are dieting while taking HCG.

STALLS IN WEIGHT LOSS

For every pound of fat, our body creates a mile of vessels just to support it. When fat is extracted from the cells of the fatty tissue all the connective tissue and blood vessels may lag behind. Your body may **hold water** while it prepares to rid you of this excess tissue. Your weight may not go down, but you have in fact lost fat.

"Patients, who have previously regularly used diuretics as a method of reducing, lose fat during the first 2 or 3 weeks of treatment which shows in their measurements, but the scale may show little or no loss because they are replacing the normal water content of their body which has been dehydrated. Diuretics should never be used for reducing."
- from 'Pounds and Inches' by Dr. Simeons

One may plateau for four to six days in the second half of the HCG Diet, especially if a person has been averaging a pound lost per day. A plateau always corrects itself. If you like, you can do an 'apple day' to break the plateau. To do this, drink only enough water to satisfy your thirst, and eat up to six apples during the day. Do this for one day. Your weight should drop by the next morning.

Whether you do an apple day or not, your weight loss will continue as long as you are not making any errors on the HCG Diet.

If you had maintained a certain weight for a long time in the past, it can take some time to break through **this past set point** in body weight.

Your weight may stay the same for 10 days or more, but if you persevere, you will break through. This is a dangerous time; the lack of weight loss can certainly test your resolve and weaken you to cheating, which will put you even further behind reaching your goal.

Another reason for a stall is one that occurs a few days before and during the **menstrual period** and possibly at ovulation. Weight loss will continue once the period is over. It is stated in 'Pounds and Inches' to not take HCG while on your cycle, this only applies to the injection method. Continue on your drops every day.

The most common reason for a stall in weight loss is **dietary error**. Even the smallest error or cheat can stall weight loss. Recheck your diet, the ingredients in the products you are using, and the weight of your raw meat. Although salt is not restricted on the HCG diet, in order for the body to accommodate one teaspoon of salt, it requires one quart of water. This equates to about two pounds of water weight on the scale!

Insufficient water intake is another reason for a stall. As soon as the body senses it does not have enough water, it will retain water.

Constipation is common in people, and not only while on the HCG Diet. Laxatives are not recommended while on the diet. Considering how little food you are taking in, a bowel movement every three days is normal. However, taking magnesium is a very healthy way to getting things 'to move along'.

Dosage is very individual. If you take too little, you won't 'go', if you take too much, have a good book in the bathroom. To find the dose that is right for you, start with one or two tablets, and work up from there.

I would like to make an extra note here, for those taking a calcium/magnesium supplement; understand that the calcium uses the magnesium in order to be made useful to the body. Taking this supplement adds little extra magnesium to your body.

Lack of Protein can cause water retention. Be sure you are eating your protein allotment.

A few people actually feel **depressed** the first week or so while on the HCG Diet. This is due to withdrawal from sugar. It has now been scientifically proven that **sugar addiction** is real and withdraw is very real – in a few days your body will break this addiction while on the diet. So, if you feel down, know what is going on and that it will only last a few days. You will feel so much better once this addiction is broken, and your body is in a healthier state.

Lastly, I would like to address **emotional eating**. Some people have a difficult time on a diet as their eating habits are largely due to emotional dependence, not hunger.

To get to the root of emotional issues, depression, anxiety or inappropriate eating, you may want to check out the **Callahan Technique.** Do a search on the Internet, and you will find a lot of information on this tapping technique.

This method sounded so odd to me at first, but there is definitely something to it. You can get a lot of information and techniques free of charge. If these issues are not addressed, your weight problem will most likely show up again in the future. Although the HCG Protocol teaches your body to maintain a healthy weight while you eat like a 'normal person', the weight will not stay off if your eating is excessive.

PHASE THREE
3-week period following the drops

This phase is critical for resetting the hypothalamus gland, which controls the endocrine system of your body.

NOTE: During this phase you do not eat sugars or simple starches. This is not a no-carb diet. You do not count calories. You do not restrict your amount of food.

The most important thing is to continue weighing yourself each morning. If your weight goes up by more than two pounds, **that very day**, do a 'steak day'. A steak day is this; eat nothing all day and then for supper, eat the largest steak you can manage, along with an apple or a tomato. If tended to promptly, the extra weight will be gone by morning.

If you lose more than two pounds, you need to eat more. You are stabilizing, teaching your body that this is your new body weight. You are teaching your body that you can **eat like a normal person** and maintain your weight.

This phase is a wonderful opportunity to change your lifestyle; your way of eating. Give up processed and fast foods. Eat more vegetables, fruits and healthy protein.

Buy a book or search out articles on the glycemic index. It is a good guide for a lifelong eating plan. It also gives you an idea of how different foods affect your blood sugar levels.

ATTENTION: If you have suffered from allergies, rheumatoid arthritis, gout, or any ailment, and found that you felt better while on the HCG Diet, I recommend you continue to keep a food journal. Take note of all of the foods you are eating, and note how they affect your symptoms. Food is often the trigger for ailments, and just like an elimination diet, you can often track down the troublemakers. You could be symptom-free for life!

TIPS FOR PHASE THREE

Continue to weigh yourself every day. Be sure to stay within two pounds less or more than your last weigh-in while on Phase Two.

Don't eat sugars or foods high in starch; this includes, in part, breads, baking, pasta, rice, potatoes, crackers, corn, winter squash, beans and cereals. Corn is right off the chart in sugar and starch, and corn has very little nutritional value. However, snow peas and baby corn used in stir-fry dishes are very low in starch.

You may have some alcohol. Dry wine, beer or hard liquor is allowed in moderation but don't use drink mixes with sugar (this includes fruit juice which has as much sugar as many sodas do), or liqueurs.

Dried fruit is very high in sugar. Some fresh fruits are very high in sugar as well; check the glycemic index so you can make good choices. Nuts are allowed, but they are high in calories, so eat them in moderation. A handful of almonds in the evening is a great nutritional choice; the natural, unroasted ones are best.

All lotions and cosmetics are allowed in Phase Three. Fats and oils are not restricted. However, as often as possible, use healthy fats like coconut oil or olive oil.

Swear off all artificial sweeteners; none of them are safe. Watch for them in low calorie products and yogurt. Speaking of yogurt, Greek yogurt is an excellent choice.

It is very high in protein. Choose plain, organic yogurt, and add your own fruit for flavorings. Most yogurts have as many calories and sugar as pudding. Read those labels!

Continue to read labels, especially avoiding corn sugar, fructose, MSG and excessive preservatives. These ingredients come disguised under many names. Refer to the information I have provided on various pages throughout this book.

PHASE FOUR
A lifestyle

This phase is when you start reintroducing some carbohydrates back into your diet.

Take any supplements you wish.

Continue to drink plenty of water, and make it part of your lifestyle.

Continue to weigh yourself daily. Make note of foods that make you gain weight. Those are the foods you will need to limit, in order to maintain your new weight.

If you gain weight, you can still do a steak day. Alternatively, you can cut the carbohydrates out of your diet for a day or two until your weight comes back into range.

Do not limit your calories enough that you are hungry. **You are no longer on a diet.** You are free to eat like a normal person, and not gain weight. Identify the foods you need to avoid but don't limit calories. You want to keep your new metabolism in top working condition!

Congratulations!
You have taken the steps to improve your health, your self-confidence, and every aspect of your life.

You deserve it!

BEVERAGES

V – 10
Makes one serving
1 vegetable per serving

Ingredients:

1 tomato, skinned and seeded	1
2 Tablespoons lemon juice	30 mL
1 teaspoon minced cilantro	5 mL
Plain Stevia to taste	
1 minced garlic clove	1
¼ teaspoon cumin	1 mL
¼ teaspoon Worcestershire sauce	1 mL
¼ teaspoon celery salt	1 mL
1/8 to ¼ teaspoon Tabasco sauce	.5 to 1 mL
Salt and pepper to taste	

Method:
Place all ingredients in a blender and puree until the mixture reaches the desired consistency. Add water if needed.

Chill in the refrigerator and serve over ice.

Health Tip:
If you cut only one thing out of your diet to increase your health, make it soda pop, regular or diet – it is all "poison" in the body. Make a permanent decision to switch to flavored water, plain water or tea. This change alone can cut your risk of metabolic syndrome by 50%! The sweetness of soda, diet or regular, makes it harder for people to stick to their efforts in maintaining a healthy weight. Consider this, most people who drink diet pop are NOT thin. And don't be fooled by canned iced tea, you would have to drink 100 cans to equal the benefits of 1 cup of homebrewed tea!

HOT APPLE CIDER
Makes 4 servings
1 fruit per serving

Ingredients:

4 apples	4
5 cups water	1250 mL
4 packets Stevia or to taste	4
1 teaspoon cinnamon	5 mL
¼ teaspoon ground cloves	1 mL
¼ teaspoon ground nutmeg	1 mL
1 teaspoon vanilla extract	5 mL

Method:
Wash and core apples and cut into quarters. Put water and apples in a saucepan and simmer for 45 minutes. Turn off heat and let cool.

Strain off the liquid apple juice and add sweetener, spices and vanilla extract to taste. Reheat cider and serve. You may eat the apple solids left over if you like.

Health Tip:
B12 is a required supplement while on the HCG diet, but you may want to continue taking it on a regular basis. B12 cuts the risk of fatigue by increasing the liver's ability to convert food into energy. Rapid detoxification can cause some fatigue and B12 will help. As B12 is easily destroyed by stomach acid, taking a sublingual tablet is preferable, 1000 mcg per day is recommended. There is no danger in taking this dose of B12, as it is a water-soluble vitamin and any B12 that is not needed by the body at the time will simply 'wash through'.

STRAWBERRY & ORANGE SHAKE
Makes 1 serving
2 fruits per serving

Ingredients:

1 cup frozen or fresh strawberries	250 mL
½ of an orange or 1/3 cup fresh juice	75 mL
¾ cup of crushed ice	175 mL
Stevia, plain or flavored, to taste	

Method:
Place all ingredients into a blender and puree until desired texture is achieved.

Serve immediately.

Health Tip:
Keep your orange peels. Place them in a dish near your work area. The scent of oranges travels through the olfactory system to stimulate your brain's limbic system – your memory center – in less than a second – helping you work more effectively.

__LEMONADE__
Makes 3 servings
Free food per serving

Ingredients:

3 cups of water	750 mL
6 Tablespoons of fresh lemon juice	90 mL
30 drops Stevia or to taste	30 drops

Method:
Mix all ingredients and serve over ice.

Health Tip:
Artificial, chemical sweeteners cause weight gain, fatigue and headaches (think about it, how many thin people drink diet pop).

Stevia is safe for diabetics as it helps balance blood sugar, which in turn reduces cravings – and that is good for anyone.

Truvia is a blend of Stevia and a natural sugar alcohol erythritol. For about 10 percent of people though, erythritol can cause mild bloat and cramping.

Stevia can leave an aftertaste that bothers some people; perhaps this blend would be something good to try.

The zest from lemons contains d-limonene, an antioxidant that helps prevent many forms of skin cancer. Make use of those peels, but be sure to wash the lemons first!

ICED TEA
Makes 4 servings
Free food

Ingredients:

4 cups water	1 litre
6 tea bags, your choice of flavor(s)	6
Stevia to taste – plain or flavored	
4 Tablespoons fresh lemon juice	60 mL
(optional)	

Method:
Bring the water to a boil. Place your choice of flavors of tea in a teapot and pour the boiling water over the tea bags. Let the tea bags steep for 10 minutes. Bob the teabags in the water to release more of the flavor of the tea.

Add the lemon juice, if desired and Stevia sweetener to taste. Stevia comes in many flavors; you may want to try some to add to the flavor.

Pour the tea into a serving pitcher over ice cubes, if serving immediately. If you are storing extra tea for later use, don't add ice until serving.

Health Tip:
People are overdosing on fluoride. Fluoride is a toxic waste product put into many municipalities' water supply and dental products, and marketed as a benefit to our teeth. Over time, fluoride can build in the body, and supplant iodine in the thyroid, making the thyroid sluggish, causing fatigue, weight gain and poor immunity. Switch to fluoride-free dental products and pure water. Use pure water when making tea, as tealeaves absorb more fluoride from soil than any other edible plant. Herbal teas have 30 times less fluoride than regular tea. Go for the Herbal!

JULIUS
Makes one serving
1 fruit per serving

Ingredients:

1 orange	1
1 cup of ice	250 mL
5 drops Stevia or to taste	5

Method:
Peel, seed and section the orange and place it in a blender.

Add the ice to the blender along with the Stevia and blend to the desired consistency. Add a bit of water if needed.

Adjust the sweetness with Stevia if needed.

Serve immediately.

Health Tip:
Our body uses vitamin C to produce collagen. You can't put a collagen cream on your face and expect any results; your skin can't use it. Better to fend of wrinkles by eating vitamin C and giving your body what it needs to protect your skin. In fact studies show that people that eat the most vitamin C have 11% less wrinkles. Oranges and strawberries are good sources of vitamin C.

STRAWBERRY LEMONADE
Makes 1 serving
1 fruit per serving

Ingredients:

1 cup frozen strawberries	250 mL
¼ cup fresh lemon juice	50 mL
1 cup ice	250 mL
10 drops lemon or plain Stevia	10

Method:
Place all ingredients into a blender and blend until it is the desired consistency.

Add a bit of water if needed and extra Stevia to taste if required.

Health Tip:
The body's ability to flush trapped fluid and toxins and metabolize stored fat peaks between 6 a.m. and noon. That makes morning the ideal time to eat fruit. You will maximize your intake of the enzymes needed to perform the fat-burning biochemical process and you won't slow your detoxification with foods that are hard to digest.

So, for those of you wanting a bit of breakfast, go for the fruit. Studies have also shown that for optimal health and prevention of disease, fruit should always be eaten by itself, on an empty stomach.

GRAPEFRUIT SPARKLER
Makes 1 serving
1 fruit per serving

Ingredients:

Juice of ½ of a grapefruit
¾ cup sparkling mineral water   175 mL
Vanilla flavored or plain Stevia to taste

Method:
Pour grapefruit juice and mineral water into a serving glass.

Add Stevia to taste.

Add ice and serve

Health Tip:
Grapefruit is an excellent source of Vitamins A, B and C, potassium, folate and fiber. The pink grapefruit is loaded with cancer-fighting lycopene. Grapefruit is in season in January and February.

Choose fruit that feels heavy for its size and has a fairly smooth skin, both of these characteristics indicates juiciness.

A half grapefruit has approximately 50 calories. Half of a grapefruit contains 76% of the RDA requirement for vitamin C!

Many prescriptions and over the counter drugs interact with grapefruit, so it is wise to take your medications or supplements 1 hour before or after eating grapefruit.

APPLE SPARKLER
Makes one serving
1 fruit per serving

Ingredients:

Juice of 1 apple   1
¾ cup sparkling mineral water   175 mL
1 Tablespoon lemon juice   15 mL
Vanilla or Carmel flavored Stevia to taste

Method:

Pour the apple juice, lemon juice and mineral water into a
serving glass. Use your homemade juice. Commercial
juice has most of the goodness processed out of it and may
have added sugar.

Add Stevia to taste. Add ice and serve.

Health Tip:
Apples have a high content of quercetin, which helps eliminate
carcinogenic (cancer causing) toxins by boosting the liver's ability to
make detoxifying enzymes. Quercetin is also proven to increase
lung function. Onions are also very high in quercetin.

A study showed that eating an apple before a meal helped people
lose 33% more weight than those who did not. Apples' soluble fiber
slows the release of sugar into the bloodstream and helps keep you
feeling full which results in eating less at meals.

LIME SPARKLER
Makes one serving
Free food

Ingredients:

3 tablespoons fresh lime juice	45 mL
¾ cup sparkling mineral water	175 mL
¼ cup fresh mint leaves	50 mL
Or	
1 Tablespoon dried mint leaves	15 mL
Plain or mint Stevia to taste	

Method:
If you are using fresh mint leaves, crush them to release the flavor.

If you are using dried mint leaves, place them in the limejuice and let sit for 15 to 30 minutes to release the flavor.

Pour limejuice and mineral water over the mint. Add Stevia to taste.

Serve immediately over ice.

Health Tip:
The flavonoid compounds responsible for the limes' fragrance have an alkalinizing effect on the body. This stimulates the production of digestive juices. Limejuice can improve your digestion.

The magnesium and calcium, plentiful in most mineral waters are both potential blood pressure reducers. In a study of people with borderline hypertension, these people experienced a significant decrease in blood pressure after 4 weeks of drinking 1 litre of mineral water per day.

DIET POP
Makes one serving
Free food

Ingredients:

1 cup sparkling mineral water	250 mL
3 Tablespoons lemon, lime or orange juice	45 mL
Plain or flavored Stevia to taste	

Method:
Mix all ingredients together and serve immediately over ice.

Mix and match different flavors for variety.

Health Tip:
Drinking as little as one sweetened beverage (anything that lists sugar, sucrose, fructose, corn syrup or fruit-juice concentrates as an ingredient) increases the risk of diabetes. Diet sodas, sweetened with chemical sweeteners are even more dangerous to overall health. Adopt this "new pop" recipe in your life as a new habit. Again, how many people that drink diet pop are thin and healthy?

Research shows that drinking 8 glasses of water (2 liters) can burn almost 35,000 calories a year, enough to help you drop 10 pounds. Once you are done this phase of the HCG diet be sure to keep up your habit of drinking water.

MOCHA COFFEE
1 milk per serving

Ingredients:

1 cup brewed hot coffee	250 mL
1 Tablespoon milk	15 mL
¼ teaspoon cinnamon	1 mL
Chocolate Stevia to taste	

Method:
Stir the milk and Stevia into the coffee and sprinkle with cinnamon

Option:
Use room temperature coffee and pour it into a blender with 1 cup (250 mL) of crushed ice or small ice cubes. Blend to desired consistency. Serve immediately.

Health tip:
Again on the MSG... it can over stimulate brain cells, especially in the hunger-regulating hypothalamus gland, triggering stress and cravings. MSG is in nearly all packaged and restaurant foods and even in some coffee served at famous franchises!

MSG reportedly was designed to fatten lab rats quickly so that obesity testing could be done on them. Once manufacturers began adding MSG to food (because they know it makes us eat more), this completely unregulated chemical has been put into our food supplies in increasing amounts. Some of its aliases: "autolyzed yeast" "calcium caseinate" "hydrolyzed protein". Watch those labels!!

BONUS SECTION!!

COFFEE can help you burn 44% more fat. Hot or cold, caffeine induces thermogenesis, a heat-producing process that jump-starts metabolism, resulting in a 44% great fat burn for 3 hours.

Plus, caffeine has been shown to diminish cravings for sweet and salty snacks by regulating the output of a hunger-causing neuro-transmitter corticotrophin-releasing hormone. Brew organic coffee to reap the benefits.

Its rich amounts of antioxidant polyphenols are proven to reduce diabetes risk by 30%; protect against heart disease, stroke, Alzheimer's disease and cancer. It also neutralizes the free radicals that cause skin to age.

Here is the breakdown according to a recent study:
1. cup of coffee per day lowers risk of early death from all causes by 37%
2. cups per day reduces risk from heart disease by 25%
3. cups per day reduces risk of dementia and Alzheimer's by 65%
4. cups per day reduces the risk of type 2 diabetes by 56%
5. or more cups per day had a 40% decreased risk of brain, larynx and mouth cancer.

Take it for what you will, but coffee has its benefits without a doubt.

These statistics do not apply to decaffeinated coffee.

Coffee speeds metabolic rate by 5% and boosts fat burn during physical activity by 31%, according to researchers. Drink coffee 30 minutes before your workout and it can increase your stamina. The caffeine stimulates steady adrenaline output and speeds blood sugar absorption by the muscle cells.

FRESHEN YOUR COFFEE POT. Here is a task that gets neglected, but it doesn't take a lot of time. Once a month, run a half pot of white vinegar and then run 2 pots of fresh water. The vinegar removes the buildup of mineral deposits that make coffee taste bitter. Brew a better coffee and help your machine last longer.

Coffee oils cling the inside of the carafe. For a fresher, better tasting coffee, wash the carafe with soap and water to cut this film.

Add a pinch of salt when brewing coffee and you will have better flavor.

For a different flavor with the added bonus of adding valuable nutrients to your coffee, sprinkle your coffee with cinnamon or nutmeg.

FILTER YOUR WATER! Home filtered water has proven to be a safer bet than most bottled water. Store water in stainless steel or glass to avoid chemical contaminants such as BPA, which can leach from plastic bottles. Using filtered water will reduce your exposure to cancer causing agents and hormone-disrupting chemicals.

FACTS ABOUT TEA YOU SHOULD KNOW

DANDELION ROOT TEA optimizes gallbladder function on several fronts. It helps break down fatty sludge in the gallbladder and stimulates bile flow for a cleansing effect. It also has an anti-inflammatory action that protects against swollen bile ducts, which impedes bile release. It is also an excellent diuretic, helping the body to release excess fluids. 1 to 2 cups per day is recommended.

TEA HAS A SHELF LIFE The level of disease-fighting antioxidants in tea bags falls by 32% after 6 months. The loose tea lasts up to a year if stored in an airtight container. Store tea in airtight containers in a cool dark place. Green tea has the shortest shelf life of all the teas.

ELIMINATE FOOT ODOR Brew some strong black tea, let it cool to a comfortable temperature and soak your feet for 30 minutes. Tea's tannins kill bacteria and close the pores in your feet, which helps keep your feet dry longer. Bacteria thrive in moisture. You will see results in a few days. Caution; don't do this if you have sores on your feet.

COOL A FEVER Sip linden flower tea. It stimulates the hypothalamus to better control your temperature and it dilates blood vessels, which induces sweating. Steep 1 Tablespoon (15 mL) of the dried herb in a cup of hot water for 15 minutes. Drink 3 to 4 cups per day.

PUFFY, TIRED EYES Black tea is full of stringent compounds called tannins and it can help deflate and tighten the bags under your eyes. Dip a tea bag in a cup of hot water for several minutes. Cool the tea bag in the fridge and apply the bag as a compress to closed eyes for 10 minutes.

DRY EYES chamomile has a mild anti-inflammatory effect. Steep a bag of chamomile in a cup of water, cool for 20 minutes until cold. Apply as a compress to your eyes for 10 minutes until the bag is room temperature.

DIARRHEA Another use for chamomile tea, drink a cup as it has an antispasmodic effect that helps stop the contractions in the lower intestine.

SOOTH A COUGH Shogaols are the compounds that give ginger its power and is more effective at suppressing cough than over the counter drugs. Grate a piece of fresh gingerroot, about as big as your thumb, into a mug and add boiling water. Steep for 5 minutes, strain and sweeten to taste.

HELP DEPRESSION People who drink 4 or more cups of green tea a day are 44% less likely to be depressed than those who don't. Its amino acid theanine helps the release of the feel-good brain chemical serotonin.

RELAX WITH EARL GREY Bergamot is the spice that give this tea its scent. Bergamot stimulates the area of your brain that promotes calm. It also contains L-theanine, an amino acid that helps promote relaxation.

TEA BLUNTS SUGAR SPIKES The polyphenols in tea help steady blood glucose after a high-carb meal (not an issue on the hcg diet – but remember this for later). Tea helps avoid belly fat, cravings and energy and mood dips that result from carb-induced blood sugar swings.

BAD BREATH Tea is a proven remedy to help bad breath.

TEA BLOCKS FAT Tea's powerful polyphenols inhibit activity of the fat-digesting enzyme lipase and this blocks the absorption of dietary fat and cholesterol in the digestive tract.

GET THE MOST FROM YOUR TEA Brew your tea for at least 5 minutes, bobbing the tea bag in the water in order to get the greatest amount of healthy benefits. If you drink your tea with a squeeze of lemon juice you can increase antioxidant levels by up to 80%. If you like tea with milk, you are better off without it – it can reduce the absorption of the tea's benefits.

HAVE TEA BEFORE MEALS If you have tea 30 minutes before every meal you could lose twice as much weight. Green tea has plant compounds that boost levels of norepinephrine, a neurotransmitter that revs your fat burn.

KEEP YOUR ENERGY UP Green tea is rich in theanine, an amino acid shown to boost alertness without producing an energy crash afterward.

Tea is proven to help lower blood pressure and cholesterol. Plus, it may offer protection against heart disease, premature aging and certain cancers. Have tea after a meal or at snack time.

SOUPS

GREEN ONION SOUP
Makes 2 servings
½ vegetable per serving

Ingredients:

10 green onions, trimmed and chopped	10
2 cups fat free vegetable broth	500 mL
1 – 2 teaspoons Braggs liquid aminos	15 – 30 mL
1 Tablespoon parsley	15 mL
½ teaspoon seasoning salt	2 mL
1 teaspoon dill	5 mL
¼ teaspoon celery salt	1 mL
¼ teaspoon chili pepper flakes	1 mL

Method:
Place all ingredients in a saucepan.

Simmer over medium heat for 20 minutes or more so the flavors of the seasonings have a chance to develop.

Serve hot.

This soup is basically a freebie on the HCG diet, a nice warm soup to even have as a snack if you need one.

Cooking Tip:
Herbs can lift a dish in taste and nutrition. Herbs such as oregano and thyme are more flavorful when dried. However, tender-leaved herbs, such as cilantro, parsley and basil are best used fresh.

CREAM OF CHICKEN SOUP
Makes 4 servings
1 protein & 1 vegetable per serving

Ingredients:

14 oz. cooked chicken breast	400 grams
3 cups chopped celery	750 mL
6 cups fat free chicken broth	1500 mL
8 cloves of minced garlic	8
3 Tablespoons minced onion	45 mL
2 Tablespoons chopped parsley	30 mL
1 Tablespoon basil	15 mL
Salt and pepper to taste	

Method:
Place all ingredients in a blender except the chicken broth. Add 2 cups of the broth and pulse blend until the soup reaches the desired consistency – adding more broth as needed.

Pour the soup mixture and all remaining broth into a saucepan and heat over medium heat for 30 minutes. Serve hot.

Alternate Method:
If you use raw chicken, simmer it in 6 cups (1500 mL) of water with all of the remaining ingredients. Let the soup cool somewhat before blending. You will probably need to blend the soup in 2 or 3 batches, depending on the capacity of your blender. Once blended, return the entire mixture to the cooking pot and reheat before serving.

HOMEMADE CHICKEN BROTH
Used for many recipes or for sautéing with

Ingredients:

3 cups of water   750 mL
7 ounces chicken breast   200 grams
Use desired amounts of the suggested seasonings:

Parsley	Celery Salt
Onion powder	Seasoning Salt
Garlic	Bragg's liquid aminos
Thyme	Sage
Rosemary	Basil
Bay Leaf	Oregano
Poultry Seasoning	Salt & Pepper

Method:
Bring all ingredients to a boil in a large pot. Lower heat and simmer for 30 minutes, the longer you simmer the broth the more flavor it will have.

Remove chicken and save for future meals. Strain the broth and chill. Skim any fat off the surface when fully chilled. Store in the refrigerator, or freeze for future use. Option: Do not use the chicken and simply make vegetable broth with this recipe.

Cooking Tip:
Freeze broth in ice cube trays. You can use one ice cube at a time for sautéing foods. If you want to make soup, the ice cubes will melt faster than if the broth was frozen in a larger container. Makes for faster and easier meals.

Fresh chopped onion and celery may be used. They will be strained out of the broth so it won't count as a vegetable serving.

SOUTH OF THE BORDER CHICKEN SOUP
Makes 4 servings
1 meat and 1 vegetable per serving

Ingredients:

14 ounces cooked chicken, shredded	400 grams
6 cloves garlic, minced	6
1 onion, chopped fine	1
4 tomatoes, diced	4
8 cups fat free chicken broth	2 Liters
½ cup fresh chopped cilantro	125 mL
1 teaspoon cumin	5 mL
1 teaspoon chili powder	5 mL
½ teaspoon cayenne pepper	2 mL

Method:

In a pot, sauté the onion and garlic in a bit of the chicken broth until slightly caramelized.

Add the broth, tomatoes, cumin, chili powder & cayenne pepper to the pot and simmer for 30 minutes.

Ladle into serving bowls and top with cilantro.

Health Tip:
Cumin has more than 100 chemicals that help ease digestion and prevent gas and bloating. It helps stimulate the enzymes that break down food so you get more nutrients. Fats and toxins are swept out of the body before they can be stored.

CURRY CHICKEN SOUP
Makes 4 servings
1 meat and 1 vegetable per serving

Ingredients:

14 ounces of cooked chicken, cubed	400 grams
2 onions, diced	2
8 cups fat free chicken broth	2 Liters
6 cloves garlic, minced	6
2 teaspoons curry powder	10 mL
1 teaspoon cinnamon	2 mL
¼ teaspoon allspice	1 mL
½ teaspoon nutmeg	2 mL
Salt and pepper to taste	

Method:
In a pot, sauté the onion and garlic in a bit of broth until slightly caramelized.

Add all remaining ingredients to the pot. Simmer for 30 minutes.

Serve hot.

Health Tip:
Diallyl sulfide and allicin are present in allium vegetables like garlic and onions. These compounds optimize the liver's ability to convert fat-soluble toxins into water-soluble substances so they can be carried out of the body.

LEMON CHICKEN SOUP
Makes 4 servings
1 meat and 1 vegetable per serving

Ingredients:

14 ounces of cooked chicken	400 grams
4 cups fresh, chopped spinach	1000 mL
Or	
2 cups frozen, chopped spinach	500 mL
½ cup lemon juice	125 mL
2 teaspoons thyme	10 mL
1 teaspoon lemon pepper	5 mL
1 teaspoon salt	5 mL
8 cups fat free chicken broth	2 Liters

Method:
Over medium heat, place all ingredients in a pot.
Simmer for 30 minutes. Adjust seasonings as desired.
Serve hot.

Health Tip:
Homemade soup is best. 92% of all canned soup tested positive for harmful bisphenol A. Prepared soups tended to be very high in sodium as well. Soups sold in cartons are usually free of BPA.

Make a large batch of soup and freeze portions for later use – most non-creamy soups freeze very well.

Soup is economical and filling, in fact, studies show that people take in 20% fewer calories in a day if soup is eaten before the main course. Beware of cream based, thick soups; they are very high in calories and fat. Again, homemade is best.

TOMATO SOUP
Makes 2 servings
1 vegetable per serving

Ingredients:

2 large tomatoes	2
2 cloves garlic, minced	2
1 cup water	250 mL
2 teaspoons basil	10 mL
½ teaspoon onion powder	2 mL
½ teaspoon salt	2 mL
½ teaspoon pepper	2 mL
Stevia if needed	

Method:

Cut tomatoes in half and place on a nonstick baking sheet, cut side down. Broil for 5 to 10 minutes until the skins are blistered and blackened. Let the tomatoes cool and remove the skins and seeds.

Pour a bit of water in a saucepan and sauté the garlic for 2 minutes. Puree the tomatoes and pour them into the saucepan. Add the remaining water and seasonings. Simmer for 10 minutes. Add Stevia if the soup is too tart. Serve hot.

Health Tip:
There are many different B vitamins – let's cover a couple of them:
B12 supplements of 1000 mcg per day correct deficiencies – susceptibility to canker sores can be a symptom of B12 deficiency.
Folate – if you are short on this vitamin you are more likely to suffer from allergies.
B Complex can cut the severity and frequency of migraines. The B vitamins lower levels of homocysteine, an amino acid that restrict blood flow to the brain. Because it lowers homocysteine, it is also good for lowering bad (LDL) cholesterol levels.

HOT AND SOUR SOUP
Makes 2 servings
1 meat and 1 vegetable per serving

Ingredients:

7 ounces raw shrimp or crab	200 grams
8 asparagus spears, snapped and chopped	8
Or	
2 cups shredded cabbage	500 mL
4 cups fat free vegetable or chicken broth	1 Litre
3 Tablespoons rice vinegar	45 mL
2 Tablespoons Braggs aminos	30 mL
½ teaspoon pepper	2 mL
½ teaspoon ground ginger	2 mL
Or	
2 teaspoons minced fresh ginger	10 mL
½ teaspoon red pepper flakes	2 mL

Method:

In a pot, mix broth, vinegar, aminos, ginger, pepper and red pepper flakes. Simmer for 15 minutes. Add the asparagus and simmer 5 minutes. If you are using cabbage instead, simmer for 10 minutes. Add the raw shrimp and simmer until the shrimp is pink and cooked through, about 5 minutes. Adjust seasoning as desired. If you find the broth too tart, add a bit of Stevia. Serve hot.

Health tip:

The ginerols and ferulic acid in ginger increase the production of bile and that in turn can reduce the intensity of acid reflux. Ginger is often taken for an upset stomach as well. It can also relieve headaches. It relaxes constricted blood vessels in the head and blocks production of pain-causing chemicals. Relax and have some ginger tea.

MEATBALL SOUP
Makes 4 servings
1 meat, 1 Melba and 1 vegetable per serving

Ingredients:

7 ounces lean ground steak	400 grams
4 Melba toast, ground fine	4
2 Tablespoons milk	30 mL
½ teaspoons onion powder	2 mL
½ teaspoon garlic powder	2 mL
½ teaspoon seasoning salt	2 mL
½ teaspoon pepper	2 mL
1 Tablespoon Braggs aminos	15 mL
8 cups fat free beef broth	2 Litres
1 onion chopped	1
3 cups shredded cabbage	750 mL

Method:

In a bowl, mix the milk, Melba, Braggs Aminos and seasonings together. Add the meat, mix well and roll into balls. Place on a nonstick baking sheet. Bake at 350°F (180°C) for 15 to 20 minutes until cooked through.

Sauté the onion in a pot with a bit of the broth until slightly caramelized. Sauté the cabbage with the onion for 2 minutes. Add the remaining broth to the pot. Add the meatballs. Simmer for 20 to 30 minutes. Serve hot.

Cooking Tip:
To make meal preparation fast and easy, make a multiple batch of meatballs, and freeze in 3 ½ ounce (100 grams) bags. The same goes for vegetable, chicken and meat broth – freeze in various sizes to suit your needs. Or, freeze broth in ice cube trays – this is very handy when you need just a bit for sautéing. Thaws quickly, too.

ONION SOUP
Makes 4 servings
1 vegetable per serving

Ingredients:

4 onions sliced thin	4
8 cups fat free beef broth	2 Liters
8 cloves garlic, minced	8
1 teaspoon black pepper	5 mL
1 teaspoon salt	5 mL

Method:

In a frying pan, sauté the onions and garlic in a bit of beef broth until caramelized. Remove the onions and garlic and put into a pot.

Put a bit more broth in the frying pan, and stir up the bits and brownings that remain. Pour the brownings into the pot. Put the remaining broth into the pot with the salt and pepper. Simmer 20 minutes and serve hot.

Health Tip:

The term 'natural flavoring' can be, but is not always, monosodium glutamate, MSG. When flavor is extracted from foods, the amino acid glutamic acid is freed. Once freed, the acid acts on, and destroys, nervous-system cells, triggering symptoms like poor concentration, headaches, mood swings, vision problems and a racing heart.

'Natural flavor' can also refer to essential oils or spice blends, which may not contain MSG. Usually, a higher price for the product will reflect true natural flavors. Sticking with whole foods and homemade food will help you avoid MSG.

Other terms to watch for are 'flavors', 'yeast extract' and 'textured vegetable protein'. No doubt manufacturers are trying to hide the fact that their products do indeed contain MSG, and the trend is more so as people become more aware of the dangers of MSG.

BEEF BROTH
Use for soups, recipes and sautéing

Ingredients:

3 cups of water	750 mL
7 ounces lean beef	200 grams

Use desired amounts of the suggested seasonings:

Parsley	Celery Salt
Onion powder	Seasoning Salt
Garlic	Bragg's liquid aminos
Thyme	Sage
Rosemary	Basil
Bay Leaf	Oregano
Poultry Seasoning	Salt & Pepper
Tarragon	Turmeric

Method:
Bring all ingredients to a boil in a large pot. Lower heat and simmer for 30 minutes or more. The longer you simmer, the more flavor you will have. Remove beef and save for future meals.

Strain the broth and chill. Skim any fat off the surface when fully chilled. Store in the refrigerator, or freeze for future use.

Health Tip:
You can boost antioxidants at any meal; herbs and spices can deliver just as much disease prevention as fruits and vegetables. The ORAC scale rates how much antioxidants are in a food, per ½ teaspoon (2 Ml), here are how the following rate:

Tarragon 155	Cinnamon 1,752	Turmeric 1,271
Oregano 1,753	Cloves 2,903	Sage 320
Thyme 127		

CHICKEN VEGETABLE SOUP
Makes 3 servings
1 meat and 1 vegetable per serving

Ingredients:

6 cups fat free chicken broth	1500 mL
10 ounces cooked chicken breast	300 grams
4 stalks celery, chopped	4
1 large onion, chopped fine	1
2 cups chopped cabbage	500 mL
2 chopped tomatoes	2
1 teaspoon oregano	5 mL
½ teaspoon poultry seasoning	2 mL
½ teaspoon seasoning salt	2 mL
Salt and pepper to taste	

Method:
Place broth, chicken, celery, onion, tomatoes and seasonings in a pot. Simmer for 20 minutes.

Add cabbage. Simmer for 15 minutes. Serve hot.

Health tip:
Yoga can lower blood pressure, blood sugar and cholesterol if practiced for 3 months, research suggests.

Yoga combines the sugar-stabilizing benefits of exercise with the powers of meditation and deep breathing. Oxygen helps fuel your fat burn, so the more efficiently you breathe, the better your results. Breathe in and out through both your mouth and nose.

Yoga that is not strenuous is a perfect activity while on or off the HCG diet.

ITALIAN FISH SOUP
Makes 4 servings
1 meat and 1 vegetable per serving

Ingredients:

14 ounces fish or seafood of choice	400 grams
4 chopped tomatoes	4
8 cups fat free chicken or vegetable broth	1 litre
½ cup fat and sugar free tomato sauce	125 mL
6 cloves minced garlic	6
1 diced onion	1
3 bay leaves	3
1 Tablespoon chopped parsley	15 mL
1 teaspoon oregano	5 mL
1 teaspoon basil	5 mL
1 teaspoon rosemary	5 mL
½ teaspoon fennel seed	2 mL
1 teaspoon Tabasco or other hot sauce	5 mL
Salt and pepper to taste	

Method:

In a food processor, grind the onion, parsley, garlic, oregano, basil, rosemary and fennel.

In a pot, add the broth, tomatoes, and tomato sauce, bay leaf and ground onion mixture. Bring to a boil and then simmer for at least 30 minutes to develop the flavor.

Add the fish or seafood and simmer until the fish is cooked. About 5 minutes. Remove the bay leaves. Add salt and pepper to taste. Add Tabasco to taste.

Serve hot.

SALADS AND VEGGIES

ORGANIC VS NON-ORGANIC

Buying organic has so many health benefits, less toxins and more nutrition. However, it can certainly add to the grocery bill! But, some produce is naturally less toxic than others, and so purchasing the non-organic version of those is okay.

Following are lists of the veggies that you ought to buy organic, and then a list of the ones that are okay to buy non-organic.

Be sure to wash all produce before cutting, peeling or eating!

BUY ORGANIC:

CELERY: 75% of celery is grown during the fall and winter and the wet conditions promote growth of bacteria and fungal diseases. Because we eat the entire stalk, it must be sprayed many times to ward off pests.

BELL PEPPERS: Technically peppers are a fruit and they have no bitter compounds to serve as built-in insect repellents. The creases provide great hiding spots for pesticides to accumulate.

SPINACH: This crinkled leaf is attacked by a variety of insects. Spinach tends to pull DDT residues out of the soil and into the leaf. These chemicals will remain in the earth for decades since they were banned.

KALE: The outer leaves are not removed before sale to prevent damage to the kale. Therefore, even the enemies of the pests that feed on kale are sprayed so that all bugs are destroyed.

POTATOES: Potatoes are sprayed 5 or more times during the growing season to protect against various pests and to ensure a good shape and size for manufacturers of potato products. After harvesting, another round of spraying occurs to ward off molds and sprouting.

At least 40 cancer causing chemicals are found in pesticides – we need to do what we can to reduce exposure! Pesticides act as estrogen in our bodies, causing hormonal imbalances, which is the last thing women need and they also chemically feminize men over time.

BUY REGULAR NON-ORGANIC:

ONIONS: onions make their own protective chemicals that discourage insects. Farmers may spray early in the season but residues are removed when the outer layer is shed during harvest.

SWEET CORN: Corn is husked before eating so that eliminates residues on the outside. However, corn is very high on the glycemic index and has little nutritional value – make this a treat, not a staple vegetable for meals.

PEAS: their pods protect the peas. However, this may not apply to the snow peas as the pods are eaten as well.

CABBAGE: Cabbage is sprayed, but the outer leaves that absorb the pesticides are discarded before sale.

EGGPLANT: The smooth surface sheds chemicals easily.

SWEET POTATO: This has built-in defenses – if it is bitten it oozes a white sap that gums up the insects. Before they are sold, they are cured at warm temperature and high humidity. This causes the skin to thicken and provides protection against damage and disease.

TIP:
You do not need to spend money on expensive 'vegetable and fruit washes'. Use a 'green' general household cleaner, and rinse well. Vinegar and water works well too, but be careful when using vinegar if you are washing tender produce that could pick up the flavor of the vinegar. Water alone is not as effective but it is better than nothing.

TACO SALAD
Makes 2 Servings
1 protein & 1 vegetable per serving

Ingredients:

2 cups chopped Romaine lettuce	500 mL
7 ounces lean ground steak	200 grams
½ teaspoon garlic powder	2 mL
½ teaspoon chili powder	2 mL
½ teaspoon onion powder	2 mL
½ teaspoon ground cumin	2 mL
½ teaspoon paprika	2 mL
1 finely diced onion	1

Method:
Cook the ground steak and onions. Drain off excess juices. Sprinkle the seasonings over the meat mixture and stir until thoroughly coated. Serve over romaine lettuce

Optional: serve with salsa

Cooking tip:
When preparing lettuce for a salad it is better to tear it into pieces than to cut it. Tearing it will allow it to separate alongside the veins of the lettuce, allowing it to retain water (less wilting) and nutrition – this way you can have lettuce ready to use and prepared ahead of time.

If you do prefer to cut your lettuce, use a plastic knife, a metal knife will cause browning.

CUCUMBER SALSA
Makes 2 Servings
1 vegetable per serving

Ingredients:

2 chopped, peeled & seeded cucumbers	2
2 chopped & seeded tomatoes	2
1 diced & seeded jalapeno pepper	1

To taste:
Chopped fresh cilantro
Salt
Limejuice

Method:
Place chopped tomatoes and cucumbers in a sieve over a bowl and allow to drain for at least 15 minutes to remove excess juices.

Toss with jalapeno pepper and season to taste.

Health Tip:
The acid in vinegar, lemon juice or limejuice helps blunt the effect of food on your blood sugar; it lowers the glycemic index of any food you use it on.

CUCUMBER APPLE SALAD
Makes 2 Servings
1 vegetable & ½ fruit per serving

Ingredients:

1 chopped apple	1
1 peeled & chopped cucumber	1
2 Tablespoons apple cider vinegar	30 mL
Season to taste with:	
Salt	
Pepper	
Green onion	

Method:

Mix apple and cucumber with the vinegar.

Season to taste

Health Tip:
People, who eat apples daily, lose more weight than those who avoid apples. Each apple has 5 grams of pectin, a soluble fiber that blocks the absorption of 90 calories of dietary fat and suppresses appetite for up to 4 hours.

CITRUS ASPARAGUS
Makes 2 Servings
1 vegetable per serving

Ingredients:

1 pound asparagus	500 grams
2 tablespoons lemon juice	30 mL
Fresh ground pepper	
Dried oregano	

Method:

Rinse the asparagus. Break off the bottoms; let them break where they want to break and all the tough part will come off.

Sauté the asparagus in a frying pan in enough water to just cover the bottom of the pan. Sauté for 2 to 3 minutes. Let the water evaporate.

Immediately sprinkle the lemon juice over the asparagus.

Season with pepper and oregano to taste.

Health tip:
Asparagus is one of the very best vegetables for de-toxing your system, especially the liver. In fact, it has even been touted as a cure for cancer. It is also very alkaline, a great benefit to the body.

SALAD DRESSING
No restrictions on use

Ingredients:

2/3 cup unfiltered apple cider vinegar	150 mL
1/3 cup lemon juice	75 mL
1 Tablespoon water	15 mL
½ teaspoon onion powder	2 mL
½ teaspoon garlic powder	2 mL
1 Tablespoon dried chives	15 mL
1 teaspoon dried parsley	5 mL
1 teaspoon dried basil	5 mL
Salt, pepper and plain Stevia to taste	

Method:

Mix all ingredients together in a container with a tight fitting lid or stopper.

Shake until mixed thoroughly. Shake before using as well.

Store in the refrigerator.

Health Tip:
Lemons are a top source of vitamin C. Vitamin C aids in the function of white blood cells that destroy invading microbes, it has also been proven to reduce levels of the immunity-sapping stress hormone, cortisol.

BAKED ONION
Makes 1 – 2 Servings
½ to 1 vegetable per serving

Ingredients:

1 medium onion   1
Salt and pepper to taste

Method:

Peel the onion.

Season with salt and pepper.

Wrap in foil

Bake for 45 minutes at 350°F (180°C)

Cooking Tip:
If onions bother your eyes, keep them in the fridge. The vapors that come off onions when peeling or chopping are reduced when they are cold. However, for longer-term storage, keep them in a cool dark place. If you store them with potatoes, they will keep longer.

STRAWBERRY CHICKEN SALAD
Makes 2 Servings
1 protein, 1 vegetable & 1 fruit per serving

Ingredients:

7 ounces cooked chicken breast	200 grams
4 cups torn lettuce	1000 mL
12 sliced strawberries	12

Dressing:

3 Tablespoons apple cider vinegar	45 mL
1 package Stevia	1
Salt and pepper to taste	

Method:

Toss lettuce and strawberries together.

Mix the dressing. Toss the dressing with the lettuce.

Top with chicken.

Health Tip:
Vinegar helps the body get rid of toxins that cause inflammation of the joints.

ROASTED ASPARAGUS
Makes 2 Servings
1 vegetable per serving

Ingredients:

1 pound asparagus	454 grams
4 cloves minced garlic	4
1 teaspoon basil	5 mL
1 teaspoon oregano	5 mL
Salt and pepper to taste	

Method:
Rinse the asparagus. Break off the tough stem ends. Place asparagus on non-stick tin foil. Sprinkle with the garlic, basil, oregano, salt and pepper. Seal the tin foil.
Roast or BBQ for 20 minutes at 350°F (180°C)

Alternate Method:
Pour ¼ cup (50 mL) of stock or water into a frying pan. Sauté the garlic for 2 minutes. Add the asparagus and simmer until it is tender crisp.

Add seasonings and cook for 1 minute more. If there is still liquid left in the pan, remove the asparagus and simmer the liquid to make a reduction sauce. Pour the sauce over the asparagus and serve immediately.

Cooking Tip:
If you are chopping garlic and fresh herbs, chop them together and the garlic won't stick to the knife, plus, your seasoning is mixed for you right on the cutting board.

MARINATED CUCUMBER SALAD
Makes 2 Servings
1 vegetable per serving

Ingredients:

1 peeled cucumber, thinly sliced	1
1 Tablespoon vinegar	15 mL
1 teaspoon dill	5 mL
1 package plain Stevia	1
¼ teaspoon salt	1 mL
Fresh ground pepper to taste	

Method:

Mix vinegar, dill, Stevia, salt and pepper.

Toss with sliced cucumbers

Cover and place in fridge for a least 1 hour before serving

Health Tip:
Adding vinegar to your food preparation has been proven to help keep blood sugar levels steady.

CHOPPED SALAD
Makes 2 Servings
1 vegetable & ½ fruit per serving

Ingredients:

2 cups chopped cabbage	500 ml
1 chopped apple	1
½ sliced English cucumber	½
½ sweet onion, chopped or sliced	½
2 stalks celery, sliced	2

Method:
Toss all prepared items together.
Toss with dressing of choice

NOTE: To keep this salad fresh in the refrigerator in order to have it on hand for multiple meals, do not add the dressing or cucumbers until serving time.

Coat the apples with lemon juice to prevent browning.

Health Tip:
Cabbage is part of the cruciferous family. It contains diindolylmethane (DIM) and Indole-3-carbinol; both compounds are effective in breaking down estrogen into safer compounds. Excess estrogen in men and women is a precursor for many diseases and promotes hormonal imbalance. We pick up excess estrogen from the many toxins in our environment and foods. A regular intake of cruciferous vegetables is highly beneficial.

APPLE SLAW
Makes 2 Servings
1 fruit per serving

Ingredients:

2 granny smith apples,
cored and cut into slivers   2
2 Tbsp. fresh squeezed lemon juice   30 mL
Dry Stevia to taste
Dried or fresh mint (optional)

Method:

Toss apple slivers with the lemon juice. Add Stevia to taste

If using mint, add just before serving

Health Tip:
If you want to eat organic foods you will notice at the grocery store that the cost of organic foods can add to your food budget considerably. But if you choose wisely, you can have the best of both worlds. Fruit with thin skins should be organic as pesticides penetrate the fruit. Fruit with thick skins have protection from pesticides, for instance, citrus fruits. But wash all fruits before eating or cutting as the knife can draw contaminants into the flesh of the fruit. You don't need a special fruit and vegetable wash, any general purpose, green cleaner will do. Wash with a green cleaner solution and rinse well. If you are not using a green cleaner, make the switch and do yourself and your earth a favor!

RADISH SALAD
Makes 1 serving
1 vegetable per serving

Ingredients:

1 cup sliced radishes	250 mL
1 Tablespoon lemon juice	15 mL
1 Tablespoon minced onion	15 mL
1 Tablespoon chopped parsley	15 mL
1 teaspoon Braggs liquid aminos	5 mL
Salt and pepper to taste	

Method:
Mix all ingredients together. Marinate in the refrigerator for one hour before serving to allow flavors to blend.

Health Tip:
What does your scale say about your brain?
If you are at a healthy weight your brain will likely be youthful as well. A study of overweight people showed that overweight people had 4% less brain tissue than normal-weight adults – the equivalent of their brains aging 8 years! A possible suggested cause of this is that high-calorie or high-fat foods clogs the arteries in the brain, restricting blood flow and therefore causing cells to shrink. Now there is motivation!!

I am often asked, "What is Braggs liquid aminos?" It is a natural and healthy soy sauce and can be purchased at some grocery chains and most health food stores.

GINGER ASPARAGUS
Makes 2 servings
1 vegetable per serving

Ingredients:

16 stalks of asparagus	16
½ cup water	125 mL
1 teaspoon fresh minced ginger root	5 mL
3 cloves of garlic, minced	3
Grated zest of 1 lemon	1
Black pepper and salt to taste	

Method:

Snap off the bottoms of the asparagus stalks, and snap the stalks in half.

Sauté the garlic and ginger, over medium heat with some of the water.

Add the asparagus to the pan with the remaining water, and simmer for approximately 5 minutes, until the asparagus is tender-crisp. Remove asparagus from the pan and place on a serving dish. Garnish with lemon zest, salt and pepper.

Simmer the remaining liquid in the pan and reduce the liquid until thickened and drizzle over the asparagus.

Health Tip:
Although no alcohol is allowed while on the HCG diet protocol, put this tip in your hat for future reference: If you eat asparagus when you drink alcohol, it can prevent hangover symptoms such as headache and nausea. Asparagus is packed with amino acids that help metabolize alcohol and the faster alcohol breaks down, the less likely you are to have a hangover.

STEAMED MUSTARD CABBAGE
Makes 2 servings
1 vegetable per serving

Ingredients:

½ head of cabbage   ½ head
2 tablespoons lemon juice   30 mL
2 teaspoons spicy mustard   10 mL
Salt and pepper to taste

Method:

Cut the cabbage into large pieces. Place in a steamer and steam 10 minutes, or until slightly tender.

Meanwhile, in a bowl, mix the lemon juice and mustard.

Place the cabbage in a bowl and add the mustard – lemon juice mixture. Toss together until the cabbage is coated.

Sprinkle with salt and pepper to taste.

Serve immediately.

Health Tip:
Mustard strengthens your viral immunity. The magic ingredient is turmeric, the yellow spice found in most mustard. It also contains antioxidants eugenol, curcumin and vanillic acid – all of which boost's the antiviral white blood cells by speeding the rate at which they divide.

FRESH GUATAMALAN SALSA
Makes 4 servings
1 vegetable per serving

Ingredients:

4 large chopped tomatoes	4
4 Tablespoons fresh cilantro	60 mL
3 jalapeno peppers, seeded	3
4 green onions	4
1 teaspoon basil	5 mL

Method:

Place the chopped tomatoes in a sieve over a bowl to allow excess juices to drain off.

Chop the cilantro, peppers and onions. Pour the drained liquid out of the bowl (you may want to save it for soup as it has nutrients). Place the tomatoes in the bowl. Add the cilantro, peppers, onions and basil and toss.

Let the salsa sit for 30 minutes at room temperature to allow the flavors to develop. This is excellent on a Melba toast!

Cooking Tip:

When choosing tomatoes, misshapen tomatoes are a good pick. They are probably organic or heirloom. A great way to get tomatoes is from gardeners with excess produce or farmer's markets – freeze them in freezer bags for future use. These will be far more nutritious than what you can purchase in the wintertime.

Cut tomatoes with a serrated knife to preserve juices. If you want to peel the tomatoes, cut an X with a paring knife on the bottom of the tomato. Dip it in boiling water for 30 seconds, and then plunge it into ice water. Starting at the cut, the peel will slip right off.

CITRUS TOMATO SALSA
Makes 2 servings
1 vegetable per serving

Ingredients:

2 large chopped tomatoes	2
1 Tablespoon lemon juice	15 mL
¼ teaspoon celery salt	1 mL
¼ teaspoon chili powder	1 mL
1 Tablespoon chopped, fresh cilantro	15 mL

Method:

Place chopped tomatoes in a sieve over a bowl to drain excess liquid.

Chop the cilantro. Mix cilantro with the lemon juice, celery salt and chili powder.

Pour the tomato liquid out of the bowl and place the tomatoes in the bowl. You can save the tomato liquid for soup if you like. It has a lot of vitamins in it.

Pour the cilantro mix over the tomatoes and toss well. Let the salsa sit at room temperature to allow the flavors to develop.

Cooking Tip:
Store tomatoes at room temperature. Their flavor gets dull and the meat gets mealy in the refrigerator.

If the tomatoes have very thin skin, do not pile them on top of each other.

Tomatoes continue to ripen, so buy only enough for the week. If your tomatoes are getting overripe and you know you won't be using them, toss them in a freezer bag and save them for a future use. This tip can save a lot of money over a year – it certainly did me!

ROASTED CELERY
Makes 2 servings
1 vegetable per serving

Ingredients:

6 stalks celery	6
½ cup fat free chicken stock	125 mL
2 Tablespoons lemon juice	30 mL
2 Tablespoons Bragg's aminos	30 mL
¼ cup finely chopped onion	50 mL
2 cloves minced garlic	2
¼ teaspoons red pepper flakes	1 mL
Salt and pepper to taste	

Method:

Wash and cut the celery into pieces about the size of your little finger. Place in a baking dish.

Mix the remaining ingredients and pour it over the celery.

Bake in a 350°F (180°C) for approximately 30 minutes until tender-crisp.

Health Tip:
People with asthma are more prone to inflamed airways after high-fat meals. It has also been found that fat-laden foods impair response to bronchodilators that are a top treatment for asthma symptoms. If you are an asthma sufferer, and find your symptoms relieved while on the HCG diet, this could be true for you - making this information life changing!

HERBED FENNEL
Makes 2 servings
1 vegetable per serving

Ingredients:

4 fennel bulbs	4
½ cup water or broth	125 mL
2 Tablespoons lemon juice	30 mL
½ teaspoon rosemary	2 mL
½ teaspoon seasoning salt	2 mL

Method:

Wash and trim fennel. Simmer for 10 minutes in broth with the rosemary. When fennel is tender, sprinkle with seasoning salt.

Serve hot.

Health Tip:

Up to 75% of salt intake is from packaged foods and restaurant foods. Cooking from scratch can eliminate excess salt in our diets. But when purchasing packaged foods, check the labels – look for a 1 – to – 1 ratio of calories to sodium or less.

For example, if a food has 150 calories per serving, it should have no more than 150 mg of sodium.

Aim to keep your sodium intake below 1500 mg a day. Counting milligrams can be tedious. So, if you cook smart and buy smart, you will be OK.

Calcium, potassium and magnesium help rid your body of excess sodium.

ROASTED TOMATO AND ONIONS
Makes 2 servings
1 vegetable per serving

Ingredients:

1 onion sliced thin	1
2 tomatoes sliced thick	2
2 garlic cloves minced	2
1 Tablespoon basil	15 mL
½ teaspoon oregano	2 mL
Salt and pepper to taste	

Method:

Line a baking pan with the onion slices. Sprinkle the garlic over the onion. Lay the tomato slices over the garlic and onions. Sprinkle the tomatoes with basil, oregano and salt and pepper.

Bake vegetables at 375°F (190°C) for 15 minutes or until it is done to your liking.

Serve hot.

Cooking Tip:

If a recipe calls for 1 Tablespoon (15 mL) of dried herb you can substitute fresh herbs with 4 times the amount. In this example, you would use 4 Tablespoons (60 mL) of fresh herbs.

If you are grinding fresh herbs it can get mushy and seeds can pop out. Add a bit of coarse salt to the herbs. The sharp crystals of the salt quickly reduce the spices.

Be sure to adjust your recipe for salt content.

SAUTEED BEET GREENS OR SPINACH
Makes 1 serving
1 vegetable per serving

Ingredients:

2 cups beet greens or spinach leaves	1000 mL
¼ cup broth or water	50 mL
2 Tablespoons lemon juice	30 mL
2 cloves of minced garlic	2
¼ teaspoon cumin	1 mL
¼ teaspoon seasoning salt	1 mL
¼ teaspoon ground pepper	1 mL

Method:
Mix the broth, lemon juice, garlic and seasonings. Pour the liquid into a hot wok. Add the greens and stir-fry until just hot and slightly wilted.

Serve hot.

Health Tip:
The fluorescent lights of the store bring out the best in spinach. Exposure to this light raises the vegetable's levels of vitamins C, K and E as well as folate. In fact, folic-acid levels almost doubled after 9 days under the lights. Fluorescent lighting mimics sunlight closely enough to trigger photosynthesis.

Spinach is loaded with vitamins and antioxidants and magnesium. In fact, it has 100% of the daily requirements for vitamins A and K in only ½ cup cooked spinach. It is also rich in iron, but the body does not use it well unless you take or eat vitamin C with it. An orange with spinach is an excellent choice to make the most of spinach's iron content.

PESTO SALAD
Makes 2 servings
1 vegetable per serving

Ingredients:

2 tomatoes, halved and sliced	2
1 Tablespoon basil	15 mL
½ red onion chopped fine	½
2 cloves minced garlic	2
1 Tablespoon lemon juice	15 mL
1 Tablespoon apple cider vinegar	15 mL

Method:

Toss all ingredients in a bowl until the tomatoes are well coated. Let the tomato mixture sit at room temperature for at least 30 minutes to allow flavor to develop.

Serve cold.

Health Tip:

The chromium in tomatoes helps balance blood sugar levels and helps regulate the body's use of glucose – thus keeping cravings to a minimum.

The pigments that give tomatoes its color are converted into vitamin A. Vitamin A enhances iodine absorption, which results in the creation of more metabolism-boosting thyroid hormones.

If your tomatoes are under ripe, place them in a paper bag. Close the bag, fold over the top and roll it down as far as you can. The paper traps in ethylene gas and that speeds ripening. It only takes a day or two for the tomatoes to ripen. I like to buy my week's worth of tomatoes at different degrees of ripeness. I choose a couple of ripe tomatoes for the day and the next and then some less ripe tomatoes for later in the week. This way, I am more likely to have tomatoes at their prime, all week.

THAI BEEF SALAD
Makes 2 servings
1 meat and 1 vegetable per serving

Ingredients:

7 ounces raw steak	200 grams
1-teaspoon red pepper flakes	5 mL
3 cloves minced garlic	3
1/2 teaspoon steak spice	2 mL
3 Tablespoons water	45 mL
1 cucumber, peeled, seeded and sliced	1
2 Tablespoons lemon juice	30 mL
2 Tablespoons chopped cilantro	30 mL

Method:
In a bowl, toss cucumber, lemon juice and cilantro. Chill.

Mix the garlic with the steak spice and rub the steak with it. Slice the steak into thin strips.

Heat water in a frying pan and add the steak strips. Stir-fry the steak until the steak is done how you like it.

Place the steak on a warm serving plate. Place the cold cucumber mix over the steak and serve hot.

Cooking Tip:
For easy chopping of cilantro or other fresh herbs, use kitchen shears. If you use a knife the leaves can stick to the knife.

Capsaicin, the compound that gives hot peppers their kick, raises your core body temperature, causing you to burn more calories. Hotter peppers have a greater effect – go as hot as you can and still enjoy your food.

CRAB AND CUCUMBER SALAD
Makes 2 servings
1 meat, 1 Melba and 1 vegetable per serving

Ingredients:

7 ounces shredded crab meat	200 grams
1 English cucumber, seeded	1
2 Tablespoons Braggs aminos	30 mL
1 Tablespoon rice vinegar	15 mL
2 teaspoons hot mustard	20 mL
½ teaspoon wasabi paste	2 mL
1 Melba toast, crushed	1

Method:

Mix the vinegar, mustard, wasabi and aminos.

Toss in the crab and cucumber. Place on a serving plate.

Sprinkle crushed Melba toast over the top and serve.

Health Tip:
Turmeric, the ingredient that makes most mustard a deep golden color can increase the production of the liver's primary detoxification enzyme Glutathione S-transferase. Glutathione is largely responsible for the immune system in the gut. Daily consumption of turmeric can increase Glutathione in just 14 days.

If you have had trauma or illness your reserves of Glutathione have been affected and taking turmeric daily can help restore your health. Turmeric can also be taken in supplement form.

ASPARAGUS FRITTATA
Makes 2 servings
1 meat, 1 vegetable per serving

Ingredients:

3 egg white	3
1 egg yoke	1
10 – 15 spears of asparagus	10 – 15
3 cloves minced garlic	3
¼ cup minced onion	50 mL
2 Tablespoons water	30 mL
1 Tablespoon chopped parsley	15 mL
½ teaspoon Tabasco sauce	2 mL
Salt and pepper to taste	

Method:
Preheat oven to 375° (190°C).

Wash asparagus and snap off the woody ends. Cut each spear into 3 or 4 pieces. In a frying pan, over medium heat, sauté asparagus and garlic until tender.

Wisk the egg whites and yolk together with the water and Tabasco sauce. Fold into the eggs the asparagus, onion, parsley and salt and pepper. Pour the egg mixture into a non-stick baking dish.

Bake 15 to 20 minutes until done.

Health Tip:
Antacids can cause levels of the stomach acid - hydrochloric acid (HCl) to fall too low. Without enough HCl, food isn't completely digested. This leads to further heartburn and constipation that causes fat-trapping waste to build up in the colon. Low HCl also slows production of fat-metabolizing bile, so consumed fat is stored instead of used for energy.

SHRIMP STUFFED TOMATO
Makes 1 serving
1 vegetable and 1 meat per serving

Ingredients:

3 ½ ounces cooked shrimp	100 grams
1 tomato	1
2 Tablespoons lemon juice	30 mL
2 Tablespoons sugar free cocktail sauce	30 mL
Salt and pepper to taste	

Method:
Chop the shrimp. Mix the shrimp with the lemon juice, cocktail sauce and salt and pepper.

Cover and store in the refrigerator if not using it right away, or double the recipe so you have it on hand for another day.

Wash the tomato and cut the top off. Scoop out the seeds. Fill the tomato with the shrimp mixture.

Health Tip:

Researchers have found that the bioflavonoids in tomatoes, when eaten daily, can reduce inflammatory compounds within 6 weeks. Inflammation can disrupt blood sugar balance and lowers the body's sensitivity to leptin, the hormone that revs metabolism and controls appetite.

Tomatoes also help with carb cravings, energy swings and excess belly fat. Its fiber is slow digesting making it a satisfying food to eat.

Tomatoes' antioxidant lycopene protects again cancer, heart disease and diabetes. Lycopene is an antioxidant proven to help reduce prostate cancer.

ALMOST ONION RINGS
Makes 2 servings
1 vegetable, 1 milk and 1 Melba per serving

Ingredients:

2 large onions sliced	2
2 Melba toast ground fine	2
2 Tablespoons milk	30 mL
½ teaspoon cayenne pepper (or less)	2 mL
½ teaspoon seasoning salt	2 mL
½ teaspoon pepper	2 mL

Method:
Preheat the oven to 450°F (230°C).

Mix the milk, cayenne, seasoning salt, pepper together to make a batter.

Place the ground Melba on a plate.

Put the rings of the onion in the batter. Coat the rings with batter. Let them sit a few minutes. If the coating slips off, recoat. Dip each ring in the ground Melba, one at a time, and place on a non-stick baking pan. You may want to use a zero-fat cooking spray.

Bake 6 minutes, turn over and bake an additional 6 minutes or until they are crispy. Serve hot.

Health Tip:
More than a billion germs can grow within 24 hours in the moist environment of an unclean sponge. Toss it in the dishwasher at every load. Or, you can place it in the microwave for a minute to kill germs. Replace your sponge every week or two or when it looks worn or discolored.

CHICKEN

ORIENTAL CHICKEN
Makes 3 servings
1 meat & ½ fruit per serving

Ingredients:

10 ounces chicken breast – skinned	300 grams
Juice of 2 oranges	
4 large, minced garlic cloves	
1 Tablespoon fresh, grated ginger root	15 mL
2 Tablespoons lemon juice	30 mL
¼ cup of water	50 mL
2 teaspoons of powdered chicken bouillon	
Base, or use your own homemade	
fat-free broth	10 mL

Method:
Cut chicken into thumb sized pieces. Preheat a frying pan over medium heat. Mix bouillon base powder with water, and pour into frying pan. Add chicken and stir fry for 5 to 10 minutes, until half cooked.

Pour orange and lemon juice over chicken. Add ginger root. Continue stir-frying until chicken is cooked through.

Remove chicken and place on a warmed dish.

If there is liquid in the frying pan, continue to cook the liquid while stirring up the bits that have stuck to the pan. If there is not enough liquid in the frying pan, add some water to the pan. This is called a reduction sauce. When liquid is reduced, pour over the chicken and serve.

SPICY MUSTARD CHICKEN
Makes 3 Servings
1 meat per serving

Ingredients:

10 ounces of skinned chicken breast	300 grams
¼ cup lemon juice	50 mL
3 Tablespoons Dijon mustard	45 mL
1 Tablespoon basil	15 mL
1 teaspoon cracked black pepper	5 mL
½ teaspoon cayenne pepper	2 mL
1 teaspoon Franks Hot Sauce	5 mL

Method:
Cut the chicken into 100 gram (3 ounce) pieces.

Mix the lemon juice, mustard, basil, pepper, cayenne pepper and hot sauce. Brush this mixture over all sides of the chicken.

Place chicken in an ovenproof dish or pan.

Bake chicken at 350° F (180°C) for 30 minutes, or until cooked through.

Health Tip:
Cayenne, as well as other hot peppers, activates the stomach's protective juices, therefore aiding digestion.

Mustard contains isothiocyanates, which inhibits cancer cell growth. We all have cancer cells in our bodies and we certainly want to inhibit them!

CHICKEN FINGERS
Makes 3 Servings
1 meat and 2 Melba toast per serving

Ingredients:

9 ounces of chicken breast	300 grams
4 Melba toast, ground fine in a blender	4
½ teaspoon garlic powder	2 mL
1 teaspoon smoked paprika	5 mL
½ teaspoon seasoning salt	2 mL
½ teaspoon pepper	2 mL

Method:
Cut chicken into finger sized pieces.

Mix together the ground Melba toast, garlic powder, paprika, seasoning salt and pepper. Coat each piece of chicken with the seasoning mix

Spray a baking sheet with a zero fat cooking spray and place chicken pieces on the sheet.

Bake chicken at 350°F (180°C) for 15 to 20 minutes until completely done.

Turn over each piece halfway through baking time.

Health Tip:
Garlic lowers cholesterol and blood pressure. It is antifungal, antibacterial and antiviral.

THAI CHICKEN WRAPS
Makes 2 Servings
1 meat & 1 vegetable per serving

Ingredients:

7 ounces cooked chicken breast	200 grams
4 large leaves of romaine lettuce	4
1 cup shredded iceberg lettuce	250 mL
1 teaspoon Balsamic vinegar	5 mL
1 teaspoon Rice Wine Vinegar	5 mL
2 teaspoons minced fresh gingerroot	10 mL
¼ cup minced onion	50 mL
1 minced garlic clove	1
Salt and pepper to taste	

Method:

In a bowl, mix the cooked chicken, vinegar, gingerroot, onion, garlic, salt and pepper.

Place chicken mixture on large, washed romaine lettuce leaves.

Top with iceberg lettuce

Roll up the romaine leaves to enclose the chicken mixture and serve.

Health Tip:

Ginger is proven to settle nausea and indigestion. It has even been shown to reduce pain. Ginger contains anti-inflammatory and analgesic compounds that mimic NSAIDs. Speaking of pain, being negative creates stress hormones that trigger inflammation. Need to feel better fast? Hum a tune and have some ginger tea.

CHICKY CHILI
Makes 5 Servings
1 meat & 1 vegetable per serving

Ingredients:

17 ounces ground chicken breast	500 grams
4 cups fat free chicken broth	1 litre
5 cloves of garlic, diced	5
2 teaspoons chili powder	10 mL
2 teaspoons Hot Sauce	10 mL
3 stalks of diced celery	3
4 diced tomatoes	4
1 large, finely diced onion	1

Method:
Put ½ cup (125 mL) of broth in a pot and bring to a simmer.

Add the chicken, onion and garlic to the broth in the pot. Cook until chicken is almost cooked.

Add the remaining broth, chili powder, hot sauce, celery and tomatoes.

Simmer until desired consistency.

Cooking Tip:
This dish is great to have on hand in the fridge. The flavor will develop and will taste even better the next day.

ROAST CHICKEN
Makes 5 Servings
1 meat & 1 vegetable per serving

Ingredients:

17 ounces of chicken breast halves	500 grams
3 large onions, sliced	3
5 cloves of garlic, quartered	5
¼ cup lemon juice	50 mL
Cracked black pepper to taste	

Method:

Spray a frying pan with no fat cooking spray.

Sauté the onions until slightly soft, and place in an oven proof dish.

Place chicken on top of onions.

Pour lemon juice over the chicken. Add pepper if desired.

Tuck garlic pieces under and around the chicken.

Cover and bake at 350°F (180°C) for 45 minutes.

Cooking Tip:
It is handy to have cooked chicken on hand. You can serve this chicken hot when you first bake it and use the planned leftovers for salad topping. This stays moist, so it is great cold.

HOT WINGS
Makes 4 Servings
1 meat & 1 milk per serving

Ingredients:

14 ounces chicken tenders	400 grams
¼ cup of milk	50 mL
1 teaspoon cayenne pepper	5 mL
1 teaspoon chili pepper	5 mL
½ teaspoon seasoning salt	2 mL
1 teaspoon paprika	5 mL
¼ teaspoon garlic powder	1 mL
¼ teaspoon onion powder	1 mL

Method:
Dip each chicken tender in milk.

Mix all spices together on a plate. Cover each chicken tender in the spice mixture. Place on a non-stick baking sheet.

Bake 10 minutes at 350°F (180°C). Turn over each piece and bake for 10 more minutes or until cooked through.

Cooking Tip:
Be sure to read labels when using or purchasing spices and condiments. It is surprising where you will find sugar and MSG. Sugar comes under many names: barley, malt, beet sugar, brown sugar, buttered syrup, cane-juice crystals, cane sugar, caramel, carob syrup, corn syrup, corn syrup solid, date sugar, dextran, dextrose, diatase diastatic, malt ethyl maltol, fructose, fruit juice, fruit juice concentrate, glucose, glucose solids, golden sugar, golden syrup, grape sugar, high-fructose corn syrup, honey invert sugar, lactose, malt syrup, maltodextrin maltose, mannitol, molasses, raw sugar .

SHAKE AND BAKE CHICKEN
Unlimited use

Ingredients:

2 Tablespoons onion powder	30 mL
¼ teaspoon ground thyme	1 mL
¼ teaspoon ground chili pepper	1 mL
¼ teaspoon ground oregano	1 mL
½ teaspoon paprika	2 mL
¼ teaspoon ground black pepper	1 mL
½ teaspoon sugar free seasoning salt	2 mL

Method:
Mix all ingredients together. Store in an air tight container or bag until ready to use.

To use: wash chicken breasts and remove all visible fat. Rub the spice mix over chicken to coat it well

Bake in the oven at 350ºF (180ºC) until cooked through – approximately 30 minutes for chicken strips and 45 minutes for chicken breast halves.

Cooking Tip:
You can use this dry rub on other meats as well or even sprinkle it on seafood while stir-frying. Rubs concentrate beneficial herbs and spices on your food and avoid added sugars and chemicals that commercial sauces contain. You may want to experiment with different flavors and incorporate this method as part of your lifestyle.

Recent studies suggest that thyme (which contains thymol oil) prevents blood clots, the cause of strokes.

KUNG PAO CHICKEN
Makes 2 Servings
1 meat per serving

Ingredients:

1 chicken breast, about 7 ounces – cut into bite sized chunks	200 grams
1 finely chopped onion	1
1 Tablespoon red chili paste	15 mL
½ teaspoon red pepper flakes	2 mL
2 cloves garlic, minced	2 cloves
2 teaspoons grated fresh ginger root	10 mL

Marinade:

¼ cup rice wine vinegar	50 mL
¼ cup fat free chicken broth	50 mL

Sauce:

½ cup fat free chicken broth	125 mL
1 teaspoon rice wine vinegar	5 mL

Method:
Mix the marinade ingredients and add to chicken. Let marinate for 30 minutes in the fridge. Once marinating is done, brown chicken over medium heat in a frying pan – about 8 minutes. Add the chili paste and toss till chicken is coated. Remove chicken from the pan and set aside on a warm plate.

Cook onion, garlic and ginger root until tender, about 3 minutes.

Place chicken back onto the frying pan with the onion mixture and cook until warmed through.

Garnish with red pepper flakes.

CAJUN STRIPS
Makes 2 Servings
1 meat per serving

Ingredients:

¼ cup fat free chicken broth	50 mL
1 Tablespoon Cajun seasoning	15 mL
7 oz. boneless chicken breast, halved	200 grams

Method:
Heat the broth in a frying pan.

Rub Cajun seasoning over the top half of the chicken and place, seasoned side down, in the frying pan over medium to high heat. Cook until almost half way cooked through.

While the chicken is cooking, liberally sprinkle Cajun seasoning over the top of the chicken. Turn the chicken over and brown the other side.

When chicken is more than half cooked, slice the breast into thick slices, about 1 inch thick. Turn the slices on their sides, cook 2 minutes, turn slices over and cook until done.

Remove chicken from the pan. Add just a bit of water to the frying pan and scrape up the bits and flavorings. Reduce the liquid to a thick sauce. Pour over the chicken or toss the chicken back into the pan and toss to coat.

Cooking tip:
You can eat this chicken as is or add it to a salad. This recipe is also good for prawns but the cooking time will be much less.

BLACKENED CHICKEN
Makes 2 servings
1 meat per serving

Ingredients:

7 oz. chicken breasts cut into finger-sized strips	200 grams
1 teaspoon paprika	5 mL
1 teaspoon chili powder	5 mL
¼ teaspoon cayenne pepper	1 mL
¼ teaspoon sugar free seasoning salt	1 mL
1 teaspoon Cajun seasoning	5 mL
½ teaspoon blackening spice	2 mL

Method:
Mix all spices together.

Toss the chicken strips with the spices.

Cook over high heat in a frying pan until blackened and cooked through.

Serve over spinach or a green salad.

Health Tip:
Spinach is high in Vitamin A & C, folic acid and potassium as well as iron. The body better absorbs the iron in spinach if you eat added vitamin C with it. A perfect companion to spinach would be an orange.

CHICKEN CUTLETS
Makes 2 Servings
1 meat & 1 ½ Melba per serving

Ingredients:

7 ounce chicken breast	200 grams
3 Melba toast, ground very fine	3
1 cup fat free chicken broth	250 mL
½ teaspoon garlic powder	2 mL
½ teaspoon paprika	2 mL
½ teaspoon poultry seasoning	2 mL
½ teaspoon onion powder	2 mL
¼ teaspoon black pepper	1 mL

Method:
Cut the chicken breast in half and then slice it horizontally. You now have 4 pieces of chicken.

Mix the ground Melba with the spices. Coat all sides of the chicken pieces with the spice mixture.

Pour ½ cup (125 mL) of broth in a frying pan and heat to a simmer. Add chicken to the broth. Cook about 5 minutes per side until cooked through. Add broth to the pan as needed as it evaporates.

Place chicken on a warm plate. Pour any remaining broth into the frying pan; stir up the seasoned bits cooked in the frying pan, and cook until the sauce is a desired thickness. Serve the sauce alongside the chicken.

Cooking Tip:
Don't bother purchasing onion salt or garlic salt. The powders are much more concentrated and more economical to purchase. It is easy and inexpensive to add your own salt.

CHICKEN WRAPS
Makes 2 Servings
1 meat & 1 vegetable per serving

Ingredients:

7 ounces cooked chicken breast cut into thin strips	200 grams
6 large cabbage leaves	6
2 garlic cloves minced fine	2
¼ cup apple cider vinegar	50 mL
1 onion diced fine	1
½ teaspoon salt	2 mL
½ teaspoon pepper	2 mL
1 Tablespoon fresh ginger minced fine	15 mL

Note: an alternative to cabbage leaves would be large romaine lettuce leaves; cooking to soften, not required.

Method:

Place cabbage leaves in boiling water until just softened. Remove from water and drain well. Cut the large vein out of the cabbage leaves, leaving two separate pieces. This will make them easier to roll up later.

Cook the onion and garlic until just softened. Add the ginger, salt and pepper, chicken and vinegar until the mixture is just warmed through.

Place the chicken filling on the cabbage leaves and roll up into a wrap.

Cooking Tip:
To easily peel ginger, use a spoon or table knife and scrape off the peel. The thin peel comes off easily and there is less waste. If you don't use ginger often enough to use it before it goes bad, peel and grate or chop it and keep it in the freezer. It isn't quite as good as fresh but it does the job, especially in cooked dishes.

ITALIAN CHICKEN
Makes 2 Servings
1 meat & 1 vegetable per serving

Ingredients:

1 cup finely chopped onion	250 mL
2 cloves of garlic finely chopped	2
3 cups chopped tomatoes	750 mL
7 ounces cooked chicken breast	200 grams
½ cup chopped fresh basil	125 mL
¾ teaspoon salt	3 mL
½ teaspoon hot sauce	2 mL

Method:
Cube the cooked chicken.

Over medium heat, sauté onion and garlic until soft. Add the tomatoes, chicken, basil, salt and hot sauce.

Reduce heat and simmer until heated through, and desired consistency is reached.

Cooking Tip:
To easily peel a garlic clove, trim off the bottom end of the clove and then crush the clove with the broad side of a chopping knife. The skin will lift off easily and the clove will be flattened to make for easy mincing.

Health Tip:
Tomatoes are a top source of lycopene, an antioxidant that helps prevent cancer. They also reduce LDL, the bad cholesterol.

BRUCHETTA CHICKEN
Makes 5 Servings
1 meat & 1 vegetable per serving

Ingredients:

1 pound boneless chicken breast	500 grams
4 garlic cloves, chopped fine	4
1 large onion, sliced thin	1
¼ cup balsamic vinegar	50 mL
¼ cup red wine vinegar	50 mL
1 large can (14 oz.) diced tomatoes	400 mL can
2 teaspoons basil	10 mL
2 teaspoons oregano	10 mL

Method:
Cut chicken breast into halves. Brown the chicken and onion in a non-stick pan, or using a fat-free cooking spray.

Add the garlic, vinegars, herbs and tomatoes to the pan.

Cover and simmer the chicken until cooked through, about 15 to 20 minutes.

Uncover and cook down the liquid until desired consistency is reached.

Cooking tip:
Planned leftovers make for easy meals. Cook extra chicken at one meal and make a new dish with it the next day. Perhaps add some chicken stock and make a soup, add it to a salad or make a wrap with a lettuce leaf. If you are prepared ahead, it makes it so much easier to stick to the plan.

When substituting fresh herbs for dried, use 4 times as much. Anytime you can use fresh herbs over dried you will have 'over the top' flavor!

CHICKEN STEW
Makes 5 Servings
1 meat & 1 vegetable per serving

Ingredients:

1 pound cooked boneless chicken breast	500 grams
4 cups fat free chicken broth	1 litre
1 teaspoon cayenne pepper	5 mL
1 teaspoon black pepper	5 mL
½ teaspoon cumin	2 mL
1 Tablespoon chili powder	15 mL
2 onions, chopped fine	2
2 cups shredded cabbage	500 mL

Method:
Cut up cooked chicken into small, bite-sized pieces.

Sauté onion and garlic in a bit of broth in a pot.

Add cayenne, pepper, cumin and chili powder and stir to coat the onion mixture.

Add cabbage, chicken and remaining broth to the pot.

Simmer until the cabbage is cooked and the broth is at the desired consistency.

Health tip:
Onions are high in allyl propyl disulfide; which lowers blood sugar and reduces glucose in the body.

CURRIED CHICKEN
Makes 2 Servings
1 meat per serving

Ingredients:

7 ounces boneless chicken breast	200 grams
1 teaspoon onion powder	5 mL
1 teaspoon garlic powder	5 mL
1 cup fat free chicken broth	250 mL
½ teaspoon sea salt	2 mL
½ teaspoon pepper	2 mL
Juice of 1 lime	1
3 teaspoons curry powder	20 mL

Method:
Cut chicken into cubes.

Mix onion, garlic, salt, and pepper and curry together and mix well with the chicken.

Pour half of the limejuice over the chicken mixture and mix. Let sit for now.

Heat the chicken broth in a frying pan. Add the seasoned chicken. Simmer the chicken in a frying pan until done.

Sprinkle the remaining limejuice over the chicken just before serving.

Health Tip:
Garlic is proven to lower cholesterol and blood pressure and well as thin blood in a healthy way. If you are on a blood thinner medication, you are not to take garlic, according to your doctor. Why? Because garlic works that well! So, why not prescribe garlic instead of rat poison, which is what a blood thinner is – now that is food for thought!

CHICKEN BURGERS
Makes 5 Servings
1 meat per serving

Ingredients:

1 pound ground chicken breast	500 grams
1 teaspoon lemon pepper	5 mL
½ teaspoon onion powder	2 mL
½ teaspoon garlic powder	2 mL
½ teaspoon mustard powder	2 mL
½ teaspoon seasoning salt	2 mL

Method:
Place ground chicken on a plate, and pat dry with paper towels.

Mix all seasonings together, and then mix with the ground chicken until very evenly distributed.

Shape into 5 patties.

Either fry the patties in a nonstick frying pan or BBQ them on a grill.

Serve with sliced tomato or cucumbers.

Health tip:
The chromium in tomatoes helps balance blood sugar levels and regulates the body's use of glucose, keeping cravings to a minimum. Chromium is a well known addition to weight loss supplements as it is proven to increase metabolism.

MEXICAN CHICKEN
Makes 5 Servings
1 meat & 1 vegetable per serving

Ingredients:

1 pound boneless chicken breast	500 grams
2 cups sugar free bottled salsa	500 mL

Method:
Pour salsa in a saucepan.

Cut chicken into 5 servings and place in saucepan with the salsa.

Heat to a simmer and continue to simmer until chicken is completely cooked.

If desired, remove chicken from the salsa and reduce any excess liquid in the salsa by simmering for a few minutes until it reaches the desired consistency.

If liquid evaporates too quickly, add a bit of water.

Health Tip:
All hot peppers, including jalapeno in salsa, contain capsicum, which raises the metabolism as much as 25%. Capsicum may also help heal stomach problems and ease arthritis pain. Choose the hottest salsa you can enjoy!

STIR FRY CHICKEN
Makes 2 Servings
1 meat & 1 vegetable per serving

Ingredients:

7 ounces chicken breast cut in strips	200 grams
½ cup chicken broth	125 mL
1 onion, sliced thinly	1
2 garlic cloves, sliced thinly	2
1 teaspoon Chinese 5 Spice	5 mL
1 package Stevia (optional)	1
4 cups cabbage, sliced thinly	1000 mL

Method:
Put 2 Tablespoon (30 mL) of broth in a heated wok, or a frying pan large enough to stir fry in.

Sauté garlic and onion in the heated broth until softened. Add 4 more Tablespoons of broth in the wok (60 mL) and add the cabbage. Stir-fry the cabbage over medium heat. Cook slightly and remove from the wok while it is still crunchy.

Add the chicken strips to the wok. Toss in the 5 spice and Stevia, and as much broth as is needed to cook the chicken through. When the chicken is cooked, put the cabbage mixture back into the wok, and stir fry just until heated.

Serve immediately.

Health Tip:
Cabbage contains anthocyanins, which are anti-inflammatory antioxidants that help prevent heart disease.

CHICKEN GRAVY
Makes 2 servings
1 Melba per serving

Ingredients:

½ cup fat free chicken broth	125 mL
2 Melba toast, ground to powder	2

Suggested seasonings:

Poultry seasoning	Salt
Thyme	Pepper
Sage	Seasoning salt
Tarragon	

Method:
Put half of the broth in a saucepan over medium heat. When broth begins to boil, whisk in the ground Melba toast.

When the mixture is smooth, whisk in the remaining broth.

Add desired seasonings.

Continue to cook, stirring constantly, until the gravy has thickened.

Health tip:
Tarragon has tannins that stimulate bile production in the liver and results in enhancing digestion and speeds up the elimination of metabolic wastes from the body.

SWEET AND SOUR CHICKEN
Makes 2 servings
1 meat and 1 vegetable per serving

Ingredients:

7 ounces chicken breast	200 grams
2 sweet onions sliced	2
4 teaspoons apple cider vinegar	20 mL
½ teaspoon Stevia, or to taste	2 mL

Method:
Cut the chicken into strips. Toss the chicken with the onion.

Place the chicken and onions in a tin foil packet.

Bake at 350°F (180°C) for 30 minutes, or until the chicken is done through.

Mix the vinegar and Stevia together and toss with the chicken. Adjust seasoning with salt and pepper as desired.

Serve hot.

Health tip:

Aspartame, Splenda and other sugar substitutes increase cravings for sweets and carbohydrates by triggering a shot-term insulin imbalance.

Stevia, a natural food taken from a tropical plant, is different. It can boost satiety by dropping post-meal insulin and blood glucose levels. This is a real bonus for diabetics!

Researchers also discovered that people who use Stevia consume about 300 fewer calories in a day – that alone is enough to drop, or keep off, up to 25 pounds in a year.

BEEF

MEAT BALLS
Makes 3 servings
1 meat, 1 Melba & 1 milk per serving

Ingredients:

10 ounces lean, ground steak	300 grams
3 Melba toast, ground fine	3
3 Tablespoons milk	45 mL
3 Tablespoons chopped parsley	45 mL
1 teaspoon onion powder	5 mL
1 teaspoon basil	5 mL
1 teaspoon oregano	5 mL
½ teaspoon garlic powder	2 mL
½ teaspoon salt	2 mL
½ teaspoon pepper	2 mL

Method:
Mix the ground Melba toast, milk, parsley, onion powder, basil, oregano, garlic powder, salt and pepper. Add this mixture to the ground beef.

Form into 1-inch meatballs. You should have about 21 meatballs. (That would be 7 per serving).

Place the meatballs on a non stick-baking sheet.

Bake at 350° f (180°C) for 15 minutes or until cooked through.

Cooking Tip:
Double or even triple this recipe. Put individual servings in freezer bags and freeze for future use. Use them in stew, soups or topped with tomato sauce.

BURGERS
Makes 3 servings
1 meat, 1 Melba, 1 vegetable & 1 milk per serving

Ingredients:

10 ounces lean, ground steak	300 grams
3 Melba toast, ground fine	3
3 Tablespoons milk	45 mL
3 Tablespoons chopped parsley	45 mL
1 teaspoon onion powder	5 mL
1 teaspoon basil	5 mL
1 teaspoon oregano	5 mL
½ teaspoon garlic powder	2 mL
½ teaspoon salt	2 mL
½ teaspoon pepper	2 mL
1 tomato	1
1 onion sliced	1
12 large lettuce leaves	12

Method:

Mix the ground Melba toast, milk, parsley, onion powder, basil, oregano, garlic powder, salt and pepper.

Add this mixture to the ground beef. Shape into 3 patties.

Grill on the BBQ or in a non-stick frying pan.

Serve with sliced tomato and onions and mustard if you like, between lettuce leaves. Use 2 lettuce leaves per side of burger so you have something substantial to hang onto.

ITALIAN STEAK
Makes 2 servings
1 meat and 1 vegetable per serving

Ingredients:

7 ounces steak, trimmed of all fat	200 grams
2 tomatoes, sliced	2
4 garlic cloves, sliced	4
2 teaspoons oregano	10 mL
2 teaspoons basil	10 mL
½ teaspoon Italian seasoning	2 mL
½ teaspoon pepper	2 mL

Method:

Place half of the tomato in a glass casserole dish.

Place the steak on top of the tomato.

Sprinkle the meat with garlic.

Place the remaining tomato slices evenly over the steak.

Sprinkle the seasonings over the tomato.

Cover and bake at 350°F (180°C) until the steak is done to your liking.

Health tip:
Omega-6 fatty acids cause inflammation and nearly double the risk of colorectal cancer. Omega 6 is in processed foods and some supplements as well. Omega-3 intake is important to create balance; good sources are leafy greens, grass-fed beef and fish.

STEAK SPICE
Multiple uses
Free food

Ingredients:

2 teaspoons onion powder	10 mL
2 teaspoons garlic powder	10 mL
1 teaspoon seasoning salt	5 mL
2 teaspoons pepper	10 mL
1 Tablespoon dry mustard	15 mL
2 teaspoons thyme	10 mL
2 teaspoons rosemary	10 mL

Method:
Mix all ingredients and keep in an airtight container.

Use as a dry rub on beef.

Health tip:
Meat that is grilled at high temperatures creates cancer-causing heterocyclic amines. Cutting down on grilling has been recommended for health reasons, but if you add rosemary and thyme to your marinade or rub, at least an hour before cooking, the antioxidant-rich spices significantly cut the HCAs.

Beef is high in iron but you will assimilate it better if you don't have coffee or tea 2 hours before or after eating beef. The polyphenols in coffee, black tea and green tea bind to iron from food and from pills, preventing them from being absorbed by the body. The same polyphenols are in caffeine-fee coffee and tea.

Eating foods rich in vitamin C also help you absorb iron. Tomatoes are a good source of vitamin C.

GREEK SEASONING MIX
Multiple Uses
Free Food

Ingredients:

2 Tablespoons dried oregano	30 mL
2 teaspoons onion powder	10 mL
2 teaspoons garlic powder	10 mL
1 teaspoon salt	5 mL
1 teaspoon pepper	5 mL
2 Tablespoons dried parsley	30 mL
1 Tablespoons dried basil	15 mL
½ teaspoon cinnamon	2 mL
½ teaspoon nutmeg	2 mL
½ teaspoon thyme	2 mL

Method:
Mix all ingredients and place in an airtight container.

Use as a rub on beef or chicken.

Health tip:
Do you like horseradish? If you do, here is some good news and bad news.

Horseradish contains 10 times more glucosinolates than broccoli. It can also block the growth of cavity-causing bacteria!

Caution though, more than 1 teaspoon (5 mL) per day can cause a sluggish thyroid, it contains chemicals that can disrupt the production of thyroid hormones when eaten in excess.

STEAK MARINADE
Makes enough to marinade 1 steak
Free food

Ingredients:

1 Tablespoon vinegar of choice	15 mL
1 Tablespoon rosemary	15 mL
3 minced garlic cloves	3
½ teaspoon hot pepper sauce	2 mL

Method:
Mix all ingredients and rub it onto both sides of a steak.

Place steak in a freezer bag and let it sit in the refrigerator overnight or longer to marinate. Flip the bag over a couple of times to ensure even flavor.

Cook as desired.

Cooking tip:
You can prepare a few steaks in this manner and place them in the freezer. While they are freezing and while they are thawing, the marinade does its work.

You can also let it sit in the refrigerator for a couple of days to further marinate.

DRY ONION SOUP MIX
Free food

Ingredients:

½ cup dehydrated minced onion	125 mL
1 Tablespoon onion powder	15 mL
1 teaspoon celery salt	5 mL

Method:
Mix all ingredients and store in an airtight container.

You may add this mixture to water, to taste, to make an onion soup.

Or, mix it into ground steak for flavor in hamburgers or meatballs.

Or, add this to other soup recipes for added flavor.

Health tip:
If you want to reduce your salt intake, here are some tips to do so and still have flavorful food:
- Vinegar and lemon juice - the acidity adds its own taste and also brings out the flavor in other ingredients.
- Tomatoes are also acidic and enhance the flavor of other foods.
- Hot peppers like jalapeno or red chilies or chili powder add punch to many foods.
- Herbs add flavor to a dish, experiment.
- Spices like cumin, ginger, nutmeg and dozens other spices add distinct flavor, as well as powerful nutrition. Spices are not just for baking.
-Himalayan sea salt is actually nutritious – it has natural minerals in it and not as much sodium.

SLOW COOKER ROAST
Makes 4 servings
1 meat per serving

Ingredients:

14 ounces lean steak or roast	400 grams
1 recipe of onion soup mix	1 recipe
1 cup fat free beef broth	250 mL
1 Tablespoon steak spice	15 mL

Method:
Use 3-½ ounces (100 gram) portion of lean steak, with all the fat trimmed away, or a small, lean roast.

Rub the meat with steak spice.

Sear the meat in a non-stick frying pan over medium-high heat till browned.

Place the meat in a slow cooker.

Mix the onion soup mix with the beef broth and pour it over the meat.

Cook on medium heat until meat is done as desired.

Cooking tip:
You can take meat straight out of the freezer and prepare it in its frozen state. Skip the browning of the meat. Cooking time will be longer. This is a great option if you are in a hurry or forgot to take something out of the freezer for the day. Cook on low and let it simmer all day, it will be very tender and supper will be ready when you get home.

MEATLOAF
Makes 3 servings
1 meat, 1 Melba, 1 vegetable & 1 milk per serving

Ingredients:

10 ounces lean ground steak	300 grams
3 Melba toast, ground fine	3
3 Tablespoons milk	45 mL
3 Tablespoons chopped parsley	45 mL
1 teaspoon onion powder	5 mL
1 teaspoon basil	5 mL
1 teaspoon oregano	5 mL
½ teaspoon garlic powder	2 mL
½ teaspoon salt	2 mL
½ teaspoon pepper	2 mL
3 Tablespoons herbed tomato paste	45 mL
3 drops of liquid smoke (optional)	3
1 Tablespoon water	15 mL
Stevia to taste	

Method:
Mix the ground Melba toast, milk, parsley, onion powder, basil, oregano, garlic powder, salt and pepper. Add to the ground steak.

Shape the seasoned meat into a loaf, and place it into a nonstick or glass baking pan

Bake at 350°F (180°C) for 20 minutes.

Meanwhile, mix the tomato paste, water, Stevia and liquid smoke. After baking the meatloaf for 20 minutes, spread the tomato paste mixture over the meat and bake for an additional 5 to 10 minutes or until the meatloaf is done.

BEEF DIPLESS
Makes 2 servings
1 meat and ½ vegetable per serving

Ingredients:

7 ounces lean steak sliced thin	200 grams
1 sliced onion	1
2 cups fat free beef broth	500 mL
4 cloves minced garlic	4
1 teaspoon thyme	5 mL
1 teaspoon pepper	5 mL
1 Tablespoon Braggs liquid aminos	15 mL

Method:
Sauté the onions and garlic in some of the broth over medium heat until tender.

Add the steak to the pan and sauté for 5 minutes.

Add the broth and seasonings to the pan and simmer until the steak is tender. Remove the steak and onions to a warm platter.

Boil the remaining broth until the liquid is reduced to a desired consistency. Pour the liquid over the steak and serve warm.

Health tip:
Scents have a powerful effect on us. Here are some ways to benefit your day with specific scents:
- Pine stimulates certain nerves that make you feel more alert.
- Cloves enhance your power of concentration and raises energy.
- Lavender decreases levels of cortisol, the stress hormone, and helps you relax.
- Frankincense eases anxiety and depression. It activates feel good receptors in the brain. It also boosts oxygen levels to the brain.

CHILI CON CARNE
Makes 2 servings
1 meat and 1 vegetable per serving

Ingredients:

7 ounces lean ground steak	200 grams
2 tomatoes	2
1 large diced onion	1
2 minced garlic cloves	2
½ cup fat free beef broth	125 mL
¼ teaspoon cumin	1 mL
¼ teaspoon pepper	1 mL
½ teaspoon hot sauce	2 mL
2 teaspoons chili powder	10 mL

Method:

Pour a bit of broth into a pan over medium heat.

Sauté the onion and garlic. Add more broth as necessary.

Add the meat to the pan and brown.

Puree the tomatoes and mix with all the seasonings. Pour mixture over the meat, and stir well.

Add the remaining broth to the pan, and simmer over low heat until the chili reaches the desired consistency.

Cooking tip:
This dish freezes well, Make a double batch and freeze in individual serving sizes for quick meals in the future. Being prepared makes this diet so much easier! Have a variety of recipes prepared in advance and stored in the freezer and thaw a few meals at a time so you have a variety on hand in the refrigerator.

BBQ SAUCE
Free Food

Ingredients:

¼ cup tomato paste	50 mL
¼ cup water	50 mL
½ teaspoon onion powder	2 mL
1 teaspoon red wine vinegar	5 mL
¼ teaspoon liquid smoke, or to taste	1 mL
½ teaspoon paprika	2 mL
½ teaspoon chili powder	2 mL
Stevia to taste	
Salt and pepper to taste	
Hot pepper sauce to taste, if desired	

Method:

Mix all ingredients in a small saucepan.

Heat sauce over low heat. Add more water if needed.

Simmer for 20 minutes to develop the flavor, stirring occasionally.

Store sauce in a container in the refrigerator.

Cooking tip:

Keep a batch of this sauce on hand for quick food preparation. Use it on steak, burgers, meatballs, meatloaf topping or chicken breast. You may want to make a double batch.

Use caution with sugar-free sauces and dressings in the marketplace. They most often use chemical sugar substitutes.

All chemical sugar substitutes are unsafe and are responsible for many serious illnesses. I recommend you stay away from them as part of your permanent lifestyle.

BEEF TACOS
Makes 2 servings
1 meat and 1 vegetable per serving

Ingredients:

7 ounces lean ground beef	200 grams
1 large diced tomato	1
½ cup diced onion	125 mL
10 large lettuce leaves	10
¼ cup water	50 mL
2 – 3 Tablespoons taco seasoning	30 – 45 mL

Method:
Brown the meat in a nonstick frying pan until done. Blot with paper towels to eliminate any excess fat.

Add the water and the taco seasoning to the meat. Mix well and continue to cook until seasoning is mixed in well, and the excess liquid has evaporated.

For each individual serving, place meat on two lettuce leaves, stacked on top of each other.

Top the meat with onions and tomatoes. Roll up like a taco.

Cooking tip:
Cold temperatures help stop most foods from going bad too quickly, but not tomatoes. Cold destroys lycopene in tomatoes, an antioxidant that lowers cholesterol levels and C-reactive protein. Cold also makes the tomatoes taste "mealy". Keep them on the counter at room temperature.

YES, WE HAVE NO SPAGHETTI
Makes 2 servings
1 meat and 1 vegetable per serving

Ingredients:

7 ounces lean ground beef	200 grams
3 tomatoes, pureed	3
1 Tablespoon basil	15 mL
1 Tablespoon oregano	15 mL
2 minced garlic cloves	2
1 large onion, diced	1
Salt and pepper to taste	
Water or beef broth as needed	
0 carb noodles	

Method:
Brown the beef in a pan until cooked. Remove from pan.

Blot the beef with a paper towel to remove any excess fat.

In the pan, with a bit of water or broth, sauté the onion and garlic until caramelized. Add the tomatoes and seasonings to the onion mixture. Add water if needed.

Put the beef in the tomato mixture. Simmer 20 minutes to develop flavor. Add water if needed, or simmer longer to reach the desired consistency.

Serve hot over noodles.

Cooking tip:
0 carb noodles are available online. I was also able to find them in an Asian market. They have 0 carbohydrates, 0 nutrition, 0 everything, but it gives you something to put your sauce on!

FISH & SEAFOOD

LEMON PEPPER FISH
Makes 2 servings
1 meat per serving

Ingredients:

7 oz white fish of your choice	200 grams
4 Tablespoons lemon juice	60 mL
5 cloves garlic, minced	5
1 teaspoon cracked black pepper	5 mL
¼ teaspoon salt	1 mL
½ teaspoon cumin powder	2 mL
¼ teaspoon turmeric	1 mL

Method:
Mix salt, pepper, cumin, garlic and turmeric in a small bowl.

Coat both sides of fish pieces with the spice mix. Cover and let marinate 30 to 45 minutes in the refrigerator.

Preheat oven to 400°F (200°C).

Place fish in a non-stick baking pan. Pour the lemon juice over the fish. Cover and bake until the fish flakes easily: depending on how thick the pieces are, about 15 to 20 minutes.

Health Tip:
Cumin has been used for centuries to prevent and ease indigestion. It contains more than 100 chemicals that prevent gas and bloating. It stimulates enzymes that help digestion and flushes out toxins from the intestines. You can also take cumin in capsule form or you can drink cumin seed tea.

The new non-stick pans are made of ceramic. If you have old Teflon pans, throw them out; they are contaminating your food with toxins.

FISH & ASPARAGUS PACKETS
Makes 2 servings
1 meat & 1 vegetable per serving

Ingredients:

7 oz whitefish of choice	200 grams
20 spears of asparagus	20
4 Tablespoons lemon juice	60 mL
2 teaspoons oregano	10 mL
Salt and pepper to taste	

Method:
Preheat oven to 400°F (200°C).

Snap the woody parts off the asparagus and wash.

Tear off two large squares of tinfoil. In the center of each square, place the asparagus. Sprinkle with salt and pepper to taste.

Place the fish pieces over the asparagus, dividing the fish evenly between the two packets.

Mix lemon juice and oregano, and pour it evenly over the fish in both packets. Fold up the foil to create a complete seal. Bake for approximately 15 minutes, until the fish flakes easily. Serve hot.

Cooking Tip:
If your fish is a bit less than fresh, soak it in milk for 15 minutes. It will take the fishy taste out, and the milk will not affect the calorie count of the fish.

To keep asparagus fresh for up to two weeks, remove ties or elastics from the asparagus, do not wash it and stand it upright in a water jug with an inch or two of water in the jug. Place in the refrigerator. It is amazing how long it will stay fresh!

GINGER SNAPPER
Makes 2 Servings
1 meat per serving

Ingredients:

7 oz. red snapper	200 grams
2 Tablespoons fresh ginger, grated	30 mL
2 Tablespoons balsamic vinegar	30 mL
3 Tablespoons white vinegar	45 mL
½ teaspoons salt	2 mL
½ teaspoons pepper	2 mL
½ lemon cut in thin wedges	½ lemon

Method:
Mix together the ginger, vinegars, salt and pepper. Pour into a non-stick frying pan. Place the fish in the vinegar mixture.

Simmer the fish for five minutes, turn and simmer until the fish flakes easily. Remove the fish from the pan; place it on a warm serving dish.

Continue to simmer the remaining liquid in the pan and reduce the liquid until it thickens. Pour it over the fish. Garnish with lemon wedges. Serve hot.

Cooking Tip:
You may want to try a different vinegar and switch up the flavor a bit. Vinegar you may want to try is Coconut vinegar. It is made from the sap of the coconut tree, rather than the nut, so it doesn't have a strong taste of coconut. It is milder and less acidic than most vinegar and contains B vitamins and amino acids. Try it in vinaigrettes or stir fries.

LOUSIANNA SCALLOPS
Makes 2 servings
1 meat per serving

Ingredients:

7 ounces raw scallops	200 grams
3 Tablespoons lemon juice	45 mL
½ teaspoon Cajun seasoning	2 mL
½ teaspoon garlic powder	2 mL
¼ teaspoon cayenne pepper	1 mL
¼ teaspoon lemon pepper	1 mL
½ cup water	125 mL

Method:

Mix the lemon juice and water. Set aside. In a separate bowl, mix the seasonings.

Pour the water mixture into a frying pan. Add the scallops. Sprinkle half of the seasoning mix over the scallops while they simmer. Turn the scallops over after 3 or 4 minutes.

Sprinkle the remaining seasoning over the scallops, and cook until the scallops are done through. Do not overcook or they will be tough. Remove the scallops to a warm dish.

Continue to simmer the liquid in the frying pan until the liquid is reduced to the desired consistency, then pour the liquid reduction over the scallops. Serve hot.

Health tip:
If you are hungry while on the HCG diet, you may take an extra dose of drops. However, you might try this...press firmly on the small indented area on your upper lip (called the philtrum) and massage in a circular motion for 2 minutes. This is the GV 26 acupressure point that calms the stomach muscle contractions that make your tummy growl.

CHILIAN SEA BASS
Makes 2 servings
1 meat per serving

Ingredients:

7 ounces of sea bass fillets	200 grams
3 cloves garlic, minced	3
3 Tablespoons lemon juice	45 mL
4 Tablespoons finely chopped cilantro	60 mL
½ teaspoon lemon pepper	2 mL
½ teaspoon seasoning salt	2 mL

Method:
Mix the garlic and cilantro and set aside. Mix the lemon pepper and seasoning salt and set aside.

Line a baking pan with foil, and place fish on the foil in a single layer. Sprinkle the garlic and cilantro over the fish. Now, sprinkle the lemon pepper and seasoning salt evenly over the fish. Lastly, sprinkle the fish with the lemon juice.

Fold the foil to seal in the fish, leaving the fish lying in a single layer.

Bake at 425°F (220°C) for 20 minutes or until the fish is done and flakes easily.

Health tip:
If you regularly fall asleep in less than 5 minutes, it is a sign you are sleep deprived. Shorting yourself on sleep is linked to many ills, including high blood pressure, because of the extra release of the stress hormone cortisol. Weight gain can result if you lack sleep because it can lower your metabolism. Lack of sleep can also increase your risk of type 2 diabetes, most likely because of weight gain. Most people need 7 hours of sleep – be sure you are getting enough.

SHRIMP KABOBS
Makes 2 servings
1 meat and 1 vegetable per serving

Ingredients:

7 ounces raw jumbo shrimp or prawns	200 grams
2 red onions, sliced thick or cut in wedges	2
10 cherry or grape tomatoes	10
½ teaspoon seasoning salt	2 mL

Method:

If using bamboo skewers soak in water for an hour before using so they don't burn up on the grill, I prefer metal skewers.

Place the shrimp, onion pieces and tomatoes on a skewer, alternating the items.

Sprinkle with seasoning salt.

Place on a preheated grill and grill until the shrimp is done. Turn a few times to ensure even cooking.

Health tip:
The chromium and allyl propyl disulfide in red onions help maintain glucose levels by increasing the amount of available insulin and facilitates an appropriate cell response.

SEAFOOD IN SAUCE
Makes 4 servings
1 meat and 1 vegetable per serving

Ingredients:

7 ounces raw shrimp	200 grams
7 ounces raw scallops	200 grams
3 cups canned crushed tomatoes	750 mL
1 teaspoon salt	5 mL
1 teaspoon red pepper flakes	5 mL
1 Tablespoon chopped parsley	15 mL
6 cloves garlic, minced	6

Method:
Sauté garlic over medium heat in a non-stick frying pan.

Add the tomatoes, salt and red pepper flakes to the garlic, and bring to a boil. Lower heat and simmer for 30 minutes to develop flavors and reduce liquid.

Add the shrimp and scallops to the tomato mixture and simmer until the seafood is done; about 5 minutes.

Serve hot, and sprinkle with parsley.

Health tip:
Within an hour of waking up, drink a glass of warm water with the juice of a fresh lemon squeezed in it. The combination of warm water and the lemon's natural fruit acids promotes peristalsis – the contractions of intestinal muscles. This speeds up the elimination of toxins.

Also, lemon's biologically active ingredient d-limonene helps the liver to break down toxins.

CITRUS FISH
Makes 2 servings
1 meat per serving

Ingredients:

7 ounces white fish	200 grams
2 Tablespoons minced onion	30 mL
3 Tablespoons lemon juice	45 mL
1 Tablespoon orange zest	15 mL
¼ cup chopped parsley	50 mL
Salt and pepper to taste	

Method:
Line a baking sheet with tin foil. Place the fish evenly on the foil.

Sprinkle the onion, lemon juice, orange zest, parsley and salt and pepper evenly over the fish.

Fold the foil to enclose the fish.

Bake at 350°F (180°C) for 10 to 15 minutes, until the fish is done and flakes easily.

Cooking tip:
If your fish is slightly freezer burned or just smells too fishy, here is the fix:
Cover the fish with milk, and let it sit for at least 30 minutes. If the fish is frozen, just let it thaw in the milk. The milk absorbs fishy and frozen flavor.

CAJUN FILLETS
Makes 2 servings
1 meat per serving

Ingredients:

7 ounces fish fillets	200 grams
Juice of ½ a lemon	
½ lemon sliced	½
2 teaspoons Cajun seasoning	10 mL
Salt and pepper to taste	

Method:
Line a baking sheet with tin foil. Lay the filets on the foil in a single layer. Sprinkle the filets with lemon juice and then season them with Cajun, salt and pepper.

Lay the lemon slices over the fish.

Fold up the tin foil to enclose the fish.

Bake at 350°F (180°C) for 10 – 15 minutes until the fish is done and flakes easily.

Health tip:
Quality proteins like eggs, whey, lean meats and fish have a high thermic effect. The body expends 5 times more calories digesting protein than it does processing fats or carbohydrates.

<u>GRILLED FISH</u>
Makes 3 servings
1 meat per serving

Ingredients:

10 ounces fish fillets	300 grams
2 Tablespoons lemon juice	30 mL
2 Tablespoons dried dill weed	30 mL
1 Tablespoon lemon pepper	15 mL

Method:
Brush the fish fillets with lemon juice.

Sprinkle the fillets evenly, on both sides, with dill and lemon pepper.

Spray the BBQ grill with non-fat cooking spray (before lighting the grill – do not do this if the flame is lit).

Place the fish on the grill and cook until it is done, about 4 minutes per side, depending on the thickness of the fillets.

Health tip:
Dill has many flavonoid components. Its essential oils are anti-congestive and antihistaminic, helping to clear respiratory distress brought on by a cold or allergies.

CRAB CAKES
Makes 2 servings
1 meat and 1 Melba per serving

Ingredients:

7 ounces crab meat	200 grams
1 garlic clove, minced	1
½ teaspoon lemon pepper	2 mL
¼ teaspoon salt	1 mL
1 teaspoon dry mustard	5 mL
2 Tablespoons chopped parsley	30 mL
2 teaspoons lemon zest	10 mL
2 Melba toast, ground fine	2

Method:
Mix the garlic, lemon pepper, salt, mustard, parsley, lemon zest and Melba toast together.

Add the crab to this dry mixture until mixed well. Form into 4 patties. Place in a non-stick frying pan and cook until heated through.

Cooking tip:
You can use a non-fat cooking spray while on the HCG diet. Just check the labels for fat content. The non-fat variety has only a small trace of fat (no more than lean meat) and due to its low fat content can be deemed "no fat".

If you are using a non-stick frying pan, avoid Teflon, it puts toxic residue into the food, especially if cooking with high heat. As the Teflon begins to wear, it contaminates the food even further. There is a newer version of non-stick cookware with a ceramic finish.

LEMON LIME WHITE FISH
Makes 2 servings
1 meat per serving

Ingredients:

7 ounces white fish fillets	200 grams
2 cloves minced garlic	2
½ teaspoon salt	2 mL
½ teaspoon lemon pepper	2 mL
1 teaspoon dill	5 mL
½ cup water	125 mL
2 Tablespoons lemon juice	30 mL
1 Tablespoon lime juice	15 mL

Method:
Mix the garlic, salt and pepper, dill, lemon and limejuice.

Marinate the fish in this mixture for 15 minutes – flip over half way through to evenly marinate.

Place fish, marinade and water in a non-stick frying pan. Cook the fish for five minutes per side, until the fish flakes easily.

Remove the fish to a warm platter and simmer the remaining liquid to reduce the volume. Pour the reduction liquid over the fish. Serve hot.

Health tip:
L-carnitine is an amino acid that transports stored fatty acids to the cells, which in turn burns fat for fuel. It also reduces hormone-induced cravings. L-carnitine is found in beef, poultry, fish, eggs, milk and cheese.

EAST INDIAN FISH
Makes 2 servings
1 meat per serving

Ingredients:

7 ounces white fish fillets	200 grams
2 Tablespoons lemon juice	30 mL
2 cloves minced garlic	2
½ teaspoon cracked black pepper	2 mL
½ teaspoon salt	2 mL
½ teaspoon cumin	2 mL
½ teaspoon turmeric	2 mL
½ teaspoon saffron	2 mL

Method:
Mix the lemon juice, garlic and spices together. Spread this mixture over the fish fillets and let stand for 30 minutes.

Place the fish in a non-stick frying pan, along with the marinade and cook 5 minutes per side until the fish flakes easily. Add water to the pan as needed to prevent sticking.

Drizzle the fish with extra lemon juice if desired and serve hot.

Health tip:
Turmeric increases the metabolism and helps the liver flush out toxins. It also reduces inflammation in fat cells and lowers blood sugar so much so it can help prevent diabetes. Turmeric also cuts risk of heart disease, protects you from cancers and can even stave off Alzheimer's. A valuable addition to any dish!

Saffron has been proven to ease depression as well as Prozac, with none of the negative side effects. Saffron, due to its chemical compound crocin can increase libido. Saffron is also available in tea and extract. It can also help regulate irregular periods.

ROSEMARY FISH
Make 1 serving
1 meat per serving

Ingredients:

3 ½ ounce fish fillet	100 grams
1 teaspoon Italian seasoning	5 mL
1 teaspoon crushed rosemary	5 mL
½ teaspoon cracked black pepper	2 mL
½ teaspoon sea-salt	2 mL
¼ teaspoon garlic powder	.5 mL

Method:

Mix the seasonings together and sprinkle the mixture evenly over both sides of the fish fillet.

In a non-stick pan, fry each side for about 5 minutes per side or until the fish is done and flakes easily. Add water as needed to prevent sticking.

Serve warm.

Health tip:
Adding garlic and rosemary to your cooking reduces heterocyclic amines (HCAs), chemicals that are created when cooking food over high heat or when cooking on the BBQ. If you love the blackened foods, adding these seasonings can protect your health.

ORANGE ROUGHY
Makes 1 serving
1 meat and 1 fruit per serving

Ingredients:

3 ½ ounce fillet of orange Roughy fish	100 grams
Juice of 1 orange	1
2 Tablespoons lemon juice	30 mL
½ teaspoon lemon pepper	2 mL
1/8 teaspoon cayenne pepper	5 mL

Method:
Place the fish in a non-stick frying pan. Pour the orange and lemon juice over the fish and then sprinkle with the seasonings.

Cook about 5 minutes per side, or until the fish flakes easily. Add a bit of water if necessary to prevent sticking.

Serve warm.

Option: You may use any white fish you like, but Roughy lends itself well to these flavors.

Health tip:
Almost half of the population is low on vitamin C. Those with the lowest levels were likelier to have a higher body mass index (BMI), larger waists and higher blood pressure than people taking enough vitamin C.

Your body uses vitamin C to fight inflammation and to build fat-burning compounds.

Many foods are excellent sources of vitamin C, citrus fruits, cauliflower, tomatoes and romaine to name just a few.

COOKED CEVICHE
Makes 4 servings
1 meat and 1 vegetable per serving

Ingredients:

14 ounces cooked shrimp or prawns	400 grams
½ cup lemon juice	125 mL
½ cup lime juice	125 mL
4 cloves finely minced garlic	4
2 jalapeno peppers, seeded and minced	2
1 onion diced fine	1
1 Tablespoon hot sauce (or to taste)	15 mL
4 tomatoes chopped	4
1 cucumber, seeded and diced	1
½ cup fresh chopped cilantro	125 mL
1 teaspoon sea salt	5 mL

Method:
Mix all ingredients in a bowl. Cover tightly and refrigerate for an hour to let the flavors develop. Store in the refrigerator. This dish will keep for a few days, and the flavor will keep getting stronger.

Health tip:
Magnesium reduces the effects of stress on the adrenals and helps the glands produce the ideal amounts of cortisol and DHEA. Magnesium is also responsible for proper muscle relaxation and the absorption of calcium.

Good sources of magnesium are cucumbers and citrus fruits. Foods you can have in the next phase that are high in magnesium are avocados, berries and watermelon, bananas, sunflower and sesame seeds. Supplementation of magnesium is highly recommended for constipation. Studies show most people are deficient in magnesium – you are most likely one of them.

TERIYAKI FISH
Makes 2 servings
1 meat per serving

Ingredients:

7 ounces fish fillets	200 grams
3 to 4 Tablespoons Braggs Aminos	45 to 60 mL
2 Tablespoons rice vinegar	30 mL
3 cloves minced garlic	3
2 teaspoons grated fresh ginger	10 mL
Stevia to taste	

Method:
In a small bowl, mix the aminos, vinegar, garlic and ginger.

Place fish in a dish, and coat both sides with the marinade. Cover and chill for at least 30 minutes, turn half way through.

In a non-stick frying pan, cook fish for about 5 minutes per side or until the fish is done and flakes easily. Add Stevia if desired to give the sweet taste of teriyaki. You may need to add a bit of water while cooking to prevent sticking. Remove the fish from the pan and place on a warmed dish.

Add a bit of water to the frying pan and simmer while stirring up the bits and flavoring left in the pan. Pour this reduced liquid over the fish and serve warm.

Cooking tip:
When marinating anything, I like to use a zip lock bag. Place the item to be marinated in the bag and pour the marinade into the bag. Be sure the item is evenly coated, then put in the fridge. Turn over the bag half way through to ensure even flavoring. You may also do this with many items at a time. Place food in separate bags into the freezer. By the time the food is thawed, it's marinated and ready to cook – a great convenience and time saver!

WASABI FISH
Makes 2 servings
1 meat per serving

Ingredients:

7 ounces white fish fillets	200 grams
2 Tablespoons Dijon mustard	30 mL
1 teaspoon wasabi paste or powder	5 mL

Method:
Mix the mustard and wasabi. If using the wasabi powder, you may need to add just a bit of water. Wasabi is very hot. You may want to use less.

Coat the fish fillets evenly on both sides with the wasabi mixture. Let the fish stand at room temperature for 15 minutes to let the flavor develop and permeate the fish.

In a non-stick frying pan, fry the fish for five minutes per side, or until the fish is done and flakes easily. You may need to add a bit of water to the pan to prevent sticking.

Serve warm.

Cooking tip:
To prevent fish fillets from sticking to a pan or BBQ grates, wrap the fillets in paper towels and chill for an hour before grilling. This helps the proteins on the fish's surface stick to one another so they bond less to the metal.

CREOLE WHITEFISH
Makes 2 servings
1 meat and 1 vegetable per serving

Ingredients:

7 ounces whitefish	200 grams
2 chopped tomatoes	2
1 minced onion	1
1 Tablespoon Cajun seasoning	15 mL
½ teaspoon Louisiana hot sauce	2 mL
½ cup water	125 mL

Method:
In a dish, mix the Cajun, hot sauce, water, tomato and onion.

Cut the fish into bite sized pieces and add to the tomato mixture. Stir all these ingredients until mixed well.

Cook over medium heat, in a non-stick frying pan until the fish is cooked through.

If the mixture gets dry while cooking, add some extra water. This dish is to be quite saucy, not dry. Serve hot.

Health tip:
Studies have shown that adding hot sauce to daily meals can speed weight loss. The capsaicin, the compound that gives hot sauce its heat, kills cravings by producing appetite-suppressing hormones. It also shrinks fat cells by helping the body make proteins that break down fat.

Hot sauce and peppers (which is what hot sauce is made of) also revs up the metabolism.

If you have a cold or allergies, capsaicin helps loosen mucus and congestion.

SHRIMP STIR FRY
Makes 2 servings
1 meat and 1 vegetable per serving

Ingredients:

7 ounces raw shrimp or prawns	200 grams
2 cups shredded cabbage	500 mL
½ cup fat free chicken broth	125 mL
1 onion sliced thin	1
2 minced garlic cloves	2
2 Tablespoons Braggs Aminos	30 mL
Salt and pepper to taste	

Method:

Preheat a wok or a deep frying pan over high heat. Add half of the broth and half of the aminos.

Add the cabbage to the wok, and stir-fry for three minutes until it is slightly cooked. Then, remove to a serving plate, and keep it warm.

Add the remaining broth and aminos to the wok, as well as the shrimp, onion and garlic. Cook until the shrimp is pink: do not overcook. Add salt and pepper to taste.

Place the shrimp mixture over the cabbage and serve warm.

Health tip:
Cabbage, cauliflower and broccoli contain a compound (glucosinolates) that activates detoxification enzymes. Studies show that this helps the liver break down and flush toxins from the body for up to 4 days after eating them!

CURRIED FISH
Makes 2 servings
1 meat and 1 vegetable per serving

Ingredients:

7 ounces fish fillets	200 grams
2 tomatoes sliced	2
3 Tablespoons lemon juice	45 mL
2 teaspoons curry powder	10 mL

Method:

Preheat broiler.

Drizzle the fish with lemon juice so that the fish is completely covered. Sprinkle the curry powder evenly over both sides of the fish, then place on the broiler, and top with the tomato slices.

Broil fish about 8 inches (20cm) from the flame, until the fish is done, and the tomato starts to blacken. Serve.

Health tip:
Some stats on the gut: It is 30 feet long. It has an independent nervous system of 100 million neurons in the small intestine; it regulates the absorption of nutrients and directs the body's immune defense. In fact, it houses ¾ of the body's immune cells.

Does your gut feel better while on the HCG diet? Overweight, eating before bedtime and high fat foods cause stomach acids to back up. Sugar and simple carbs causes yeast overgrowth. You are getting healthier!

CURRIED SHRIMP
Makes 1 serving
1 meat and 1 vegetable per serving

Ingredients:

3 ½ ounces shrimp	100 grams
1 small onion sliced	1
2 garlic cloves sliced	2
2 Tablespoons water	30 mL
½ teaspoon curry powder	2 mL
¼ teaspoon cumin	1 mL
Salt and pepper to taste	

Method:
Place the garlic, onion and water in a non-stick frying pan. Sauté until tender.

Add the shrimp to the pan with the curry and cumin. Cook until the shrimp is pink. Add a bit more water if needed.

Add salt and pepper to taste.

Serve warm.

Health tip:
Hunger can strike in mid afternoon. This is a great time to take a dose of B12. Have a hot cup of tea and inhale the scent of mint. The scent of mint suppresses natural appetite. You can certainly take an extra dose of the HCG drops as well. Many people enjoy their serving of fruit at breakfast and then the second selection of fruit in the mid afternoon. It doesn't matter when you eat your fruit – whatever works best for you.

FRUITS & DESSERTS

FRUIT – ORGANIC OR NOT?

Buying organic is a healthy way to go, but it certainly can increase the grocery budget! **Following is a list of fruits that are clean enough without going organic.**

Be sure to wash all produce before peeling and cutting:

Avocado: Most of the pesticides that are used accumulate only on the peel.

Pineapple: Most spraying is done early in the season so there is little residue by harvest and you have to remove the thick peel anyway.

Mangoes: These are mostly grown in Mexico, the Caribbean and South America. The dry climate discourages fungus and hand weeding is more common than the use of herbicides. Again, the thick peel is removed before eating.

Kiwifruit: Any pests that like to feed on kiwifruit are taken care of by other insects.

Cantaloupe: Although these are sprayed the rind is thick enough to protect the fruit.

Watermelon: Again, this has a thick rind as well.

Grapefruit: Although fungicides are used to control mold, most of the residues are on the peel

Honeydew Melon: Some melons are washed in diluted chlorine before packing to prevent rot, but again, thick rind, you are OK

These fruits are worth buying organic:

Peaches: These are sprayed weekly and the fuzz can trap pesticides. If you don't buy organic fruit, be sure to peel it.

Strawberries: These are very prone to disease, especially fungus. Strawberries are heavily treated just to get them to the store in decent shape.

Apples: They are susceptible to more than 30 insects and 10 diseases. Many fungicides and chemicals are added after picking as well to prevent blemishes that can accumulate during storage of up to 9 months.

Blueberries: With the increase in production comes the need for more chemicals. Berries are targets for insects and are always treated with pesticides.

Nectarines: Like a peach without the fuzz, it is attacked by the same insects and requires the same chemicals. They don't retain as many pesticides as peaches but they are more susceptible to rot and scarring.

Cherries: Are prone to fruit fly, just one in a box can destroy them all. To prevent losing crops and getting produce to the store, cherries are heavily treated.

Imported grapes: Grapes that are transported long distances are heavily sprayed with fungicides so they don't rot and split before getting to the store. Domestic table grapes do not need the same treatments – if grapes are grown in a dry climate they don't get sprayed in this manner. Check where the grapes are from.

It basically sorts out like this…. if you eat the skin on the produce, you should buy it organic.

BAKED APPLE
Makes 1 Serving
1 fruit per serving

Ingredients:

1 apple	1
¼ teaspoon cinnamon	1 mL
¼ teaspoon ground nutmeg	1 mL
¼ teaspoon ground allspice	1 mL
2 teaspoons water	10 mL
1-teaspoon vanilla extract	5 mL
Stevia to taste - optional	

Method:
Preheat the oven to 350°F (180°C).

Core the apple, leave about 1 inch of apple in the bottom of the hole. Do not core all the way through the apple. Place in a baking dish. Fill the hole in the apple with water and the spices. Add Stevia if desired.

Pour ½ cup water (125 mL) around the apple. Extra spices may be added to this water if desired.

Bake for 45 minutes until cooked through. Add the vanilla to the cooking liquid and pour over the apples. Serve hot.

Health Tip:
Apples are at their peak from September to November. Apples pack a lot of vitamin C and cancer-fighting antioxidants as well as more fiber than a bowl of bran cereal. Keep them in the refrigerator so they don't go soft.

APPLESAUCE
Makes 2 servings
1 fruit per serving

Ingredients:

2 apples	2
5 Tablespoons water	75 mL
Cinnamon to taste	
Stevia to taste	

Method:
Peel, core and dice the apples. Place in a heavy saucepan, and add the water.

Simmer the apples over medium heat until the apples are very tender. Stir often and add additional water, if necessary. If the apples are too watery at the end of the cooking time, just cook longer until the excess water is evaporated. You won't overcook the apples when making applesauce.

When the apples are fully cooked, about 30 minutes, mash or blend to desired consistency. Add the cinnamon and Stevia to taste.

Serve warm or cold. Store in the refrigerator.

Health Tip:
Fruits and vegetables can be high in pesticides and pesticides turn into phytoestrogens in our bodies, disrupting all hormonal levels – one of the results of which can be weight gain. To help the liver flush out pesticides, add dandelion greens to your salads or drink dandelion tea.

STRAWBERRY SORBET
Makes 2 servings
1 fruit per serving

Ingredients:

2 cups strawberries, washed and hulled	500 mL
1/3 cup lemon juice	75 mL
Water as needed	
Stevia to taste	

Method:
Freeze the strawberries for about 1 hour, or just start with frozen strawberries.

Put strawberries in a blender with the lemon juice and water as needed. Blend until mixture is pureed. Add Stevia to taste. Place mixture back in the freezer until the sorbet has firmed up.

Options: Instead of strawberries, you can use 2 Tablespoons (30 mL) of lemon juice and the juice of an orange (or use the whole orange and puree it) Serve frozen.

Cooking Tip:
Frozen strawberries are a great bargain; they are picked at optimum ripeness and then frozen. No strawberries going bad on the counter, just take what you need out of the bag.

If you are choosing fresh strawberries, a wonderful treat when in season, choose the smaller organic ones. Large conventionally grown berries have pesticides in and on them. They are large because they have been grown with fertilizers, and they are often woody and tasteless. This is one area where choosing organic is very important and the taste will be very rewarding as well. Purchase them in bulk from a farmer's market when in season and freeze them.

DRIED APPLE SLICES
Makes 3 servings
1 fruit per serving

Ingredients:

3 apples	3
½ teaspoon cinnamon	2 mL
Powdered Stevia to taste	

Method:

Wash and core the apples. Slice thinly. Place on a cookie sheet on parchment paper.

Sprinkle evenly with cinnamon and Stevia.

Bake at 300° (150°C) until apples are dried and chewy.

Health Tip:
Studies show that the aroma of cinnamon boosts blood flow and gives you more energy and brainpower. Cinnamon also helps regulate blood sugar levels and lower cholesterol. Cinnamon is also anti-bacterial – if you wound yourself in the kitchen, sprinkle cinnamon on the wound.

The peel of an apple contains nearly all of the fruit's quercetin, an antioxidant that helps fend off some cancers.

APPLE DIPPING SAUCE
Makes 1 serving
1 fruit per serving

Ingredients:

1 apple, washed, cored and sliced	1
3 Tablespoons lemon juice	45 mL
1 teaspoon apple cider vinegar	5 mL
1 teaspoon cinnamon	5 mL
¼ teaspoon nutmeg	1 mL
Plain for flavored Stevia to taste	

Method:
In a small saucepan, heat the lemon juice, vinegar and spices until hot. Add Stevia to taste. Pour into a small bowl suitable for dipping.

Serve with apple slices.

Health Tip:
Vinegar's acetic acid switches on genes that are key to the manufacture of fatty acid oxidation enzymes. It helps block the storage of incoming dietary fat and breaks down existing body fat. Apple cider contains potassium, an alkalinizing mineral that neutralizes internal acidity as it is metabolized and in turn heightens cell sensitivity to glucose-regulating insulin.
Potassium can flatten belly bloat by flushing retained water from tissues and helps normalize muscle contractions to prevent aches and bring down blood pressure.
Apple cider also contains acetobacter, a beneficial microbe; which binds to illness-causing bacteria in the body. This can boost defenses against infections.
Your best source of apple cider is unfiltered and unpasteurized, shake it before using. The recommended amount is 2 Tablespoons per day (30 mL).

BROILED GRAPEFRUIT
Makes 1 serving
1 fruit per serving

Ingredients:

½ grapefruit
Powdered Stevia to taste
Cinnamon to taste
Salt

Method:
Using a grapefruit knife, loosen all grapefruit sections. Place the sections in bowl. Save the peel.

Toss sections with Stevia and cinnamon and put the grapefruit sections back into its peel. Sprinkle lightly with salt, more Stevia and cinnamon if desired.

Broil for about 4 minutes until it is caramelized. Serve hot.

Health Tip:
Another reason to get sugar out of our lives, a study shows that a single serving can reduce the power of large white blood cells that take care of viruses and bacteria, for 5 hours after consumption. Sugar creates an excess of blood glucose, which latches on to white blood cells and disrupts their function.

However, Stevia does not elevate blood sugar at all! Its compounds steviol and isosteviol actually enhance the ability of muscle cells to absorb excess glucose.

APPLE CRISP
Makes 2 servings
1 fruit, 1 milk and 1 Melba per serving

Ingredients:

Filling:2 apples	2
Juice of 1 lemon	1
2 Tablespoons water	30 mL
½ teaspoon cinnamon	2 mL
Stevia to taste	

Topping:	
2 Melba toast, ground fine	2
2 teaspoons milk	10 mL
1 teaspoon cinnamon	5 mL
½ teaspoon nutmeg	2 mL

Method:
Preheat oven to 375° (190°C).

Peel, core and slice the apples and place in a baking dish.

Mix the lemon juice, Stevia and water and pour it over the apples.

In a separate bowl, mix the ground Melba toast, milk, cinnamon and nutmeg until it forms a crumbly topping. Sprinkle the topping over the apples.

Bake 20 to 30 minutes until apples are tender and the topping is crisp.

SPICED ORANGES
Makes 1 serving
1 fruit per serving

Ingredients:

1 orange, peeled and sliced	1
2 Tablespoons lemon juice	30 mL
Dash of cinnamon	
Dash of nutmeg	
Sprinkle of Stevia	

Method:
Mix spices with the lemon juice.

Warm it in a saucepan. Add the orange slices and simmer on low heat for a couple of minutes until the oranges are warm.

Place on a serving dish and sprinkle with Stevia if desired.

Health Tip:
Vitamin C can lower levels of the stress hormone cortisol a well as destroy free radicals that damage molecules. Eating 3000 mg of vitamin C can help keep you calm during stressful events.

Orange peels provide d-limonene, a compound that may protect against skin cancer. Wash the peels and finely chop – you can save them in a baggie in the freezer and use them as you need – use your imagination and add them to your favorite recipes.

BREADS

GRISSINI (Thin Bread Sticks)
1 stick per Melba serving
This recipe makes 64 bread sticks

Note: *In Dr. Simeon's book, 'Pounds and Inches', he mentions Grissini. Melba toast has been widely substituted for the Grissini, due to availability. This homemade variety is better than prepackaged, as it has no preservatives. Plus, you can change the flour options and flavoring options to suit your tastes and health needs.*

Grissini and/or Melba is allowed on the HCG protocol.

Ingredients:

2 teaspoons instant yeast	10 mL
1-½ teaspoons salt	7 mL
2 Tablespoons olive or coconut oil	30 mL
2 ¾ cup flour	675 mL
1 ¾ cup warm water	425 mL

Toppings of choice or a mixture of toppings:
Kosher salt; coarse ground pepper; chopped fennel seed are suggestions from the original recipe.

Option: use any flour or mixture of flours you choose. Amaranth, Kamut and Spelt are high protein options. This recipe can be made with gluten free flour as well.

Method:
Mix the flour, yeast and salt in a bowl.

Mix the warm water and oil in a liquid measuring cup. This liquid should be warmer than room temperature but not hot. The warmth of the liquid actives the yeast.

Put the flour mixture in a food processor. Add the liquid mixture to the flour and process about 2 minutes until the dough is smooth and elastic. Or, you could slowly mix the liquids with the dry ingredients and knead the dough until smooth and elastic.

Line a baking sheet with parchment paper.

Preheat the oven to 350°F (180°C).

Divide the dough into 4 equal pieces. Each piece will be handled the same.

On a floured surface or pastry cloth, roll the dough into a rectangle measuring about 8 X 12 inches. Cut the dough into 16 strips of equal width. A pizza cutter works well for this.

Fold each strip over on itself lengthwise. Strips will now be half the width. Now roll the strip to make each strip round, like a long thick straw. Roll these strips to be a bit longer than your baking sheet as they will shrink while baking.

Place each strip on the parchment lined baking sheet.

Lightly spray the strips with no fat cooking spray or lightly brush with egg white. Sprinkle on your chosen toppings.

Bake for 25 to 30 minutes until golden brown.

Cool on a rack. Store in an airtight container.
Note: although oil is not allowed while on the HCG protocol, there has been allowance made for the Grissini or Melba toast. This recipe is compliant to the HCG protocol. If you read the label on the Melba box, you will see oil listed.

MELBA TOAST
Makes 4 Melba toast per slice of bread
1 Melba serving per piece

Note: You may make as many Melba as you like at one time so you have them on hand. The method outlined here is per slice of bread. Choose your bread to suit your taste and health needs.

Method:
Toast bread.

Cut the slice of bread lengthwise (from top to bottom).

Stand each piece of bread up on edge and slice it into 2 thin pieces. A bread knife is best for this job. Day old bread is easier to handle than fresh bread.

You now have four pieces of toast that are untoasted on one side. Place the toast on a baking sheet with the untoasted side up.

Bake at 350°F (180°C) on the center rack for five minutes.

After five minutes, check the toast often, they will not brown equally, the thinner pieces will brown faster. Remove the pieces individually as they brown.

To determine the calorie count and fiber count of your Melba toast, check the label on your bread bag and divide by 4. This will vary widely between brands of bread.

To choose good bread, check the label, you are looking for whole grains, few preservatives, a high fiber count and a low carbohydrate count, again, brands vary widely.

WHAT'S THE BIG DEAL ABOUT HFCS?

The companies that make high fructose corn syrup (HFCS) haven't let up in their TV advertising. They're still out there claiming their chemically produced concoction is the same as natural sugar.

The corn it's made from isn't even 'natural' any more. According to the U.S. Department of Agriculture, 86% of all corn grown in America is genetically engineered.

The enzymes needed to make the high fructose corn syrup are also genetically modified. And this enzyme application is an extra processing step that even refined sugar doesn't go through.

Another extra step used to make high fructose corn syrup is to use caustic soda in the processing. The problem is, this stuff can get contaminated with mercury.

In one study, half of the HFCS samples tested had mercury. Mercury was also found in a third of the off-the-shelf commercial foods where HFCS is the first or second labeled ingredient.

The danger with HFCS is not just how it's processed or where it comes from. It's what your body does with it after you consume it.

Natural fructose occurs in the fiber of fruit. Because it's locked in the fiber, it normally absorbs into your

---

bloodstream slowly, giving your liver time to release it gradually as glucose, the sugar your body uses for energy.

HFCS literally floods your bloodstream, overwhelming your liver's processing capacity. This can lead to liver damage not unlike the kind that afflicts alcoholics.

Animals given a diet high in HFCS suffer severe cirrhosis of the liver—scarring, dead tissue, and poor liver function. Their livers look a lot like those of hardcore alcoholics.

And, your pancreas – the organ that produces insulin – really isn't designed to handle high doses of concentrated fructose.

In one study, researchers bathed human pancreatic cancer cells in both fructose and glucose. Fructose worked just as well to make cancer cells spread quickly. Not only that, but fructose triggered the expression of a certain enzyme that made both sugar sources more readily available to the cancer cells.

Other research has suggested that dietary fructose may also boost your risk of developing pancreatic cancer in addition to feeding it. One study found that people with pancreatic cancer had 2.5 times more fructose in their blood than people without it.

And now there's a brand new study showing that concentrated fructose like HFCS can even affect babies in the womb.

In an animal study done in New Zealand, researchers fed pregnant mothers high levels of fructose to see how their babies would develop. The mothers got overweight, and were producing too much insulin.

The female babies from the fructose-fed mothers were well on their way to being diabetic. They all produced too little insulin, and had high blood sugar.

The male babies also suffered from producing too little insulin. But they had an additional problem. They had high levels of BHB (beta-hydroxybutyrate). This is a chemical your body produces for energy in your brain when you can't process sugar the right way. You make it when your brain is starving.

Besides brain starvation and diabetes, there are other effects you suffer from HFCS. That's because the corn used to make the sweetener might be genetically modified. Fructose is also known to break down ATP, the molecule that gives you energy. In fact, when they want to test nutrients that will give you more energy, they use concentrated fructose like HFCS to first degrade your ATP stores.

Unfortunately, because it's so cheap to produce and easy to add to foods, HFCS is showing up in foods you might not imagine needed to be sweetened. Stove Top stuffing, Starbuck's frappuccinos, cough syrup, cottage cheese, and baked beans... the list goes on.

Chemically produced corn syrup is one of the best arguments I can think of for eating foods the way they occur naturally – or as close as you can get these days.

Anything with cane sugar is going to be better than something with HFCS. Your body is made to be able to handle foods with natural sugar. Just help your body out by choosing foods that, if they have sugar, are low on the glycemic index (GI).

This report was used by permission from Dr. Sears.

http://www.alsearsmd.com/

BONUS HORMONE REPORT

Hormonal test results have a wide berth of 'normal'. It is important for you to monitor your own symptoms – they can tell you more than preliminary tests. The following list is merely a guideline summary and is not intended as medical advice.

NOTE:

While on the HCG Diet, many of the following foods mentioned are not allowed, however, some are. Concentrate on the allowed foods. In the next phases of your diet you can begin to add these other foods to combat unbalanced hormones.

Avoidance of toxins in the first place is a great place to start! Use green cleaners, buy organic produce, and avoid plastic containers and bottles unless they are BPA free. Avoid canned food when possible as the lining of the cans contribute to estrogen overload, purchase food in glass when possible. There is so much we can do to improve our health if we are aware of what is hurting us.

Low Thyroid: (regulates many aspects of the body)
- Symptoms – depression, fatigue, poor memory, dry skin, hair loss, constipation, weight gain, thinning of the outer edge of eyebrows.
- Causes – yoyo dieting, stress, peri-menopause, menopause, pesticides.
- What can help? – Selenium – it helps manufacture active thyroid hormone.
- Sources of Selenium – walnuts, Brazil nuts, wheat germ, whole grains, pork, tuna, salmon.

Low Progesterone: (a female hormone)

- Symptoms – cravings, low libido, PMS, insomnia, anxiety, fat gain in belly, hips and thighs.
- Causes – stress, birth control pills, smoking, secondhand smoke, pesticides, and toxins from plastic.
- What can help? – Indole-3-carbinol stimulates detoxifying enzymes that flush competing hormones from the body.
- Sources of Indole-3-carbinol are broccoli, cauliflower and cabbage.

Low Testosterone: (the male hormone)

- Symptoms – weak muscles, blue mood, fatigue, low motivation, low sex drive, belly fat.
- Causes – the acne medication Accutane, elevated blood sugar, lack of weight bearing exercise.
- What can help? – Niacin – it increases HDL (the good cholesterol), which is the building block of testosterone.
- Sources of Niacin – dairy, eggs, fish, lean meats, poultry

Elevated Cortisol: (a stress hormone linked to abdominal fat)

- Symptoms – insomnia, fatigue, frequent infections, high blood pressure, low libido, increased hunger, cravings for comfort food and belly fat.
- Causes – chronic stress, unresolved anger, skipping meals, excess sugar or caffeine, yo-yo dieting.
- What can help? – Vitamin C increases the adrenals' resistance to stress and prevents cortisol spikes. Drink plenty of water.
- Sources of Vitamin C are cantaloupe, citrus fruits, strawberries and watermelon.

Elevated Insulin: (the hormone that tells the body to store excess blood sugar as fat and prevents stored fat from being burned as energy)
- Symptoms – facial hair, fatigue, cravings, mood swings, irregular periods, severe menopause, belly fat.
- Causes – eating artificial sweeteners, pesticides, stress, and toxins from plastic, history of infections.
- What can help? – Magnesium regulates insulin production and increases cells' sensitivity to insulin.
- Sources of Magnesium are Swiss chard, spinach, black beans, walnuts and quinoa.

Elevated Leptin: (a chemical messenger that reduces hunger)
- Symptoms – hunger, high cholesterol, high blood pressure, joint aches from inflammation
- Causes – perimenopause, menopause, stress, food additives, history of infections, and smoking.
- What can help? – Omega-3 fats drops leptin and increases the body's sensitivity to leptin.
- Sources of Omega-3 are salmon, tuna, sardines, fish oil, and flaxseed and chia seed.

Elevated Estrogen: (a female hormone)
- Symptoms – weight gain, especially in the hips, thighs and belly.
- Causes – excess fat, the more fat you carry the higher your estrogen levels as fat cells make estrogen.
- What can help? – Weight loss. Increase dietary fiber as it binds to excess estrogen.
- Sources that help rid you of excess estrogen are broccoli, cabbage, white beans and Brussels sprouts.

Low Serotonin: (the feel good brain chemical)
- Symptoms – low energy and mood. Poor quality of sleep
- Causes – history of antidepressants, lack of sleep
- What can help? – Get more sleep. Supplement with B12.
- Sources: eat pumpkin seeds, peanuts, fish, eggs and cheese.

Low HGH: (the human growth hormone)
- Symptoms – weight gain, poor muscle tone, skin that appears older than it is.
- Causes – lack of protein
- What can help? – Increase your intake of quality protein, quality sleep and muscle building exercises.
- Sources are all meats, fish and seafood. Pork is the lowest on the scale for useable protein by the body.

Low Glucagon: (a hormone that tells the body to burn fat when there is no blood sugar to use a fuel)
- Symptoms – excess weight regardless of diet and exercise
- Causes – eating foods that are high in carbohydrates, especially processed foods, foods based on refined grains and simple sugars.
- What can help? – Eat protein with every snack and meal. Refer to a glycemic index to get familiar with how food affects your blood sugar.
- Sources of protein are all meats, fish and seafood. Most nuts have a good balance of fats, carbs and protein.

Low Gaba: (a brain chemical responsible for calm and restful sleep.)
- Symptoms – anxiety and sleeplessness, a racing mind
- Causes – poor diet, stress and illness.

- What can help? - Inhaling the scent of Jasmine triggers the nerve to activate GABA receptors. Rub onto wrists and temples 20 minutes before bedtime.
- Raise progesterone levels by eating yams and soy (be sure soy is organic – non organic soy is heavily treated with chemicals).
- Take a L-theanine supplement of 200 mg, an amino acid.
- Take a good quality B-complex vitamin, if you don't feel a difference, change brands.

Note:

Hormone imbalances can be difficult for even a doctor to detect. Blood tests have a very wide range of normal. Your symptoms and the sense that something is wrong could be your first indication that there is indeed an imbalance. With some trial and error you can improve your health with foods and supplements.

However, medical help for serious problems is recommended.

BONUS ARTICLE

I am including this article posted on the Internet by Dr. Sears. This article will not only give you a better idea as to what is good to eat during Phase Three, (the 3 weeks following the cessation of drops) but an excellent guideline for a lifestyle way of eating.

Dr. Sears also promotes his PACE exercise system, a quick way to gain fitness and maintain a healthy weight. If you are interested in a fast and effective workout routine, I recommend you search PACE online.

What is the Glycemic Index (GI)?
The Glycemic Index (GI) is one the best tools for fat loss. It measures how quickly foods breakdown into sugar in your bloodstream. High glycemic foods turn into blood sugar very quickly. Starchy foods like potatoes are a good example. Potatoes have such a high GI rating; it's almost the same as eating table sugar.

What is the Glycemic Load (GL)?
The GI tells you how fast foods spike your blood sugar. But the GI won't tell you how much carbohydrate per serving you're getting. That's where the Glycemic Load is a great help. It measures the amount of carbohydrate in each serving of food. Foods with a glycemic load under 10 are good choices—these foods should be your first choice for carbs. Foods that fall between 10 and 20 on the glycemic load scale have a moderate affect on your blood sugar and should be eaten in moderation.

Foods with a glycemic load above 20 will cause blood sugar and insulin spikes. Try to eat those foods sparingly – save these foods as an occasional treat.

Food	Glycemic Index	Serving Size (g)	Glycemic Load
CANDY/SWEETS			
Honey	87	2 Tbs	17.9
Jelly Beans	78	1 oz	22
Snickers Bar	68	60g (1/2 bar)	23
Table Sugar	68	2 Tsp	7
Strawberry Jam	51	2 Tbs	10.1
Peanut M&M's	33	30 g (1 oz)	5.6
Dove Dark Chocolate Bar	23	37g (1 oz)	4.4
BAKED GOODS & CEREALS			
Corn Bread	110	60g (1 piece)	30.8
French Bread	95	64g (1 slice)	29.5
Corn Flakes	92	28g (1 cup)	21.1
Corn Chex	83	30g (1 cup)	20.8
Rice Krispies	82	33g (1.25 cup)	23
Corn pops	80	31g (1 cup)	22.4
Donut (lrg glazed)	76	75g (1 donut)	24.3
Waffle (homemade)	76	75g (1 waffle)	18.7
Grape Nuts	75	58g (1/2 cup)	31.5
Bran Flakes	74	29g (3/4 cup)	13.3
Graham Cracker	74	14g (2 sqrs)	8.1
Cheerios	74	30g (1 cup)	13.3
Kaiser Roll	73	57g (1 roll)	21.2
Bagel	72	89g (1/4 in.)	33
Corn tortilla	70	24g (1 tortilla)	7.7
Melba Toast	70	12g (4 rounds)	5.6
Wheat Bread	70	28g (1 slice)	7.7
White Bread	70	25g (1 slice)	8.4
Kellogg's Special K	69	31g (1 cup)	14.5
Taco Shell	68	13g (1 med)	4.8
Angel food cake	67	28g (1 slice)	10.7
Croissant, Butter	67	57g (1 med)	17.5
Muselix	66	55g (2/3 cup)	23.8
Oatmeal, Instant	65	234g (1 cup)	13.7
Rye bread, 100% whole	65	32g (1 slice)	8.5
Rye Krisp Crackers	65	25 (1 wafer)	11.1
Raisin Bran	61	61g (1 cup)	24.4
Bran Muffin	60	113g (1 med)	30
Blueberry Muffin	59	113g (1 med)	30
Oatmeal	58	117g (1/2 cup)	6.4
Whole wheat pita	57	64g (1 pita)	17
Oatmeal Cookie	55	18g (1 large)	6
Popcorn	55	8g (1 cup)	2.8

Pound cake, Sara Lee	54	30g (1 piece)	8.1
Vanilla Cake and Vanilla Frosting	42	64g (1 slice)	16
Pumpernickel bread	41	26g (1slice)	4.5
Chocolate cake w/chocolate frosting	38	64g (1 slice)	12.5

BEVERAGES

Gatorade Powder	78	16g (.75 scoop)	11.7
Cranberry Juice Cocktail	68	253g (1 cup)	24.5
Cola, Carbonated	63	370g (12oz can)	25.2
Orange Juice	57	249g (1 cup)	14.25
Hot Chocolate Mix	51	28g (1 packet)	11.7
Grapefruit Juice, sweetened	48	250g (1 cup)	13.4
Pineapple Juice	46	250g (1 cup)	14.7
Soy Milk	44	245g (1 cup)	4
Apple Juice	41	248g (1 cup)	11.9
Tomato Juice	38	243g (1 cup)	3.4

LEGUMES

Baked Beans	48	253g (1 cup)	18.2
Pinto Beans	39	171g (1 cup)	11.7
Lima Beans	31	241g (1 cup)	7.4
Chickpeas, Boiled	31	240g (1 cup)	13.3
Lentils	29	198g (1 cup)	7
Kidney Beans	27	256g (1 cup)	7
Soy Beans	20	172g (1 cup)	1.4
Peanuts	13	146g (1 cup)	1.6

VEGETABLES

Potato	104	213g (1 med)	36.4
Parsnip	97	78g (1/2 cup)	11.6
Carrot, raw	92	15g (1 large)	1
Beets, canned	64	246g (1/2 cup)	9.6
Corn, yellow	55	166g (1 cup)	61.5
Sweet Potato	54	133g (1 cup)	12.4
Yam	51	136g (1 cup)	16.8
Peas, Frozen	48	72g (1/2 cup)	3.4
Tomato	38	123g (1 med)	1.5
Broccoli, cooked	0	78g (1/2 cup)	0
Cabbage, cooked	0	75g (1/2 cup)	0
Celery, raw	0	62g (1 stalk)	0
Cauliflower	0	100g (1 cup)	0
Green Beans	0	135g (1 cup)	0
Mushrooms	0	70g (1 cup)	0
Spinach	0	30g (1 cup)	0

FRUIT

Watermelon	72	152g (1 cup)	7.2
Pineapple, raw	66	155g (1 cup)	11.9
Cantaloupe	65	177g (1 cup)	7.8
Apricot, canned in light syrup	64	253g (1 cup)	24.3
Raisins	64	43g (small box)	20.5
Papaya	60	140g (1 cup)	6.6
Peaches, canned, heavy syrup	58	262g (1 cup)	28.4
Kiwi, w/ skin	58	76g (1 fruit)	5.2
Fruit Cocktail, drained	55	214g (1 cup)	19.8
Peaches, canned, light syrup	52	251g (1 cup)	17.7
Banana	51	118g (1 med)	12.2
Mango	51	165g (1 cup)	12.8
Orange	48	140g (1 fruit)	7.2
Pears, canned in pear juice	44	248g (1 cup)	12.3
Grapes	43	92g (1 cup)	6.5
Strawberries	40	152g (1 cup)	3.6
Apples, w/ skin	39	138g (1 med)	6.2
Pears	33	166g (1 med)	6.9
Apricot, dried	32	130g (1 cup)	23
Prunes	29	132g (1 cup)	34.2
Peach	28	98g (1 med)	2.2
Grapefruit	25	123g (1/2 fruit)	2.8
Plum	24	66g (1 fruit)	1.7
Sweet Cherries, raw	22	117g (1 cup)	3.7

NUTS

Cashews	22		
Almonds	0		
Hazelnuts	0		
Macadamia	0		
Pecans	0		
Walnuts	0		

DAIRY

Ice Cream (Lower Fat)	47	76g (1/2 cup)	9.4
Pudding	44	100g (1/2 cup)	8.4
Milk, Whole	40	244g (1 cup)	4.4
Ice Cream	38	72g (1/2 cup)	6
Yogurt, Plain	36	245g (1 cup)	6.1

MEAT/PROTEIN

Beef	0		
Chicken	0		
Eggs	0		
Fish	0		
Lamb	0		
Pork	0		

Veal	0
Deer-Venison	0
Elk	0
Buffalo	0
Rabbit	0
Duck	0
Ostrich	0
Shellfish	0
Lobster	0
Turkey	0
Ham	0

Follow these tips for Fat Busting Meals:

- Avoid grains, including corn.
- Avoid potatoes and other white foods, like white rice, sugar and regular table salt.
- Try making protein the focus of each meal. It kicks your metabolism into higher gear. All meats, fish and poultry are the real 'guilt-free' foods. The protein will help you handle insulin better, build muscle and repair tissue-all essential for staying lean and preventing diabetes.
- Snack on nuts and seeds. They are a good source of protein and have Omega 3's.
- Avoid processed foods, trans fats, caffeine, and high fructose corn syrup. All increase insulin resistance.
- Choose vegetables that are low on the glycemic scale.
- Choose fruits such as berries and fruits you can eat with the skin on.
- Eat a high protein breakfast every morning. It will stabilize your blood sugar and get you off to a good start.

To Your Good Health,
Al Sears, MD

The modern health industry and big business do a lot of advertising, advising and talking about how good for you whole grains are. And now everyone seems to have fallen for the whole-grain lie. Even the smart people at Harvard.

What they should be warning you about are the whole grains.

The whole idea behind eating a grain 'whole' is this: Your body breaks down dietary starch – carbohydrates – into **glucose**, spiking your blood sugar. If a grain is left whole, you won't break it down as fast, and it won't raise your blood sugar. It sounds like a nice theory, but it doesn't work in the real world. Let me show you what I mean.

Pure glucose has a glycemic index rating of 100.

The glycemic index measures how quickly food breaks down into glucose in your bloodstream. And the higher a food's rating is on the glycemic index, the more it raises your blood-sugar level.

Here are the glycemic index ratings for one serving of some common whole-grain breads:

Whole grain bread (generic) – 51
Whole barley kernel bread – 55
Cracked wheat kernel bread – 58
Whole rye kernel bread – 66
Oat bran bread – 68

Here are the glycemic index ratings for a serving of some common snacks:
Potato chips – 54
Snickers candy bar – 55
Coca Cola – 55
Ice cream – 61
Corn chips – 63

I'm not showing you this to advise you to replace your whole grains with junk food. I'm saying whole grains ARE junk food … at least when it comes to the glycemic index. Even table sugar is only 61 on the glycemic index.

The bottom line here is that big business wants you to keep eating grains. They're cheap to produce and companies make a fortune selling grain for all those rolls, boxes of cereal and loaves of bread. None of them are natural in that you could not have eaten these processed foods in your native environment. And none of them are 'healthy'.

Real health foods are the ones you were designed to eat in your native environment: muscle and organ meat from animals and fish, and every kind of fruit, vegetable and nut. If it comes packaged in a cardboard box, plastic bag, foil wrapper or Styrofoam container, be careful of what's in there.

Here are **five tips** for shopping at the grocery store, so you can stay away from fake 'health' food like whole grains:

1. It's a good idea to stick to the outermost aisles of the grocery store, and don't eat the processed stuff they sell in the middle aisles. These are loaded with carbs, artificial sweeteners and preservatives.

2. Choose good quality protein – it is 'guilt-free' food. It won't raise your blood sugar. Grass-fed beef, free-range poultry, cage-free eggs, and wild salmon are all good choices. And, all nuts have a glycemic index of zero, except for cashews, which are a 22 on the glycemic index.

3. Choose vegetables low on the glycemic index. Those that grow above ground are good choices – cabbage, broccoli, cauliflower, asparagus, mushrooms, green beans, leafy green vegetables and tomatoes. Potatoes, which grow below ground, are 104 on the glycemic index.

4. Eat fruits such as berries and those you can eat with the skin on. Cherries, plums, peaches, strawberries and grapes, for example. Also, skip dried fruit and fruit juices (they have added sugar).

Al Sears, MD
http://www.alsearsmd.com/

CONCLUSION

All knowledge and information comes from somewhere. I could not even begin to list the sources of my information. I have been gathering it for years, and will continue to gather it and study it.

Examples of my sources of information are Internet articles, magazines, health books, and the many newsletters I subscribe to.

So, unfortunately, I am unable to give credit where credit may be due. I am grateful for the many sources of information and research that is available to us all.

One particular source I would like to mention and give credit to is Dr. Al Sears – he is a wealth of health information and offers excellent supplements as well. *http://www.alsearsmd.com/*

With all of the assaults on our environment and food supply it is our responsibility to be informed and protect the health of our loved ones and ourselves.

It is my desire that this compiled book of recipes and information is a benefit to all who use it.

Watch for the release of my next recipe book for Phase Three and onward. You can expect the same easy-to-use recipes for the everyday cook, along with more cooking and health tips, and bonus reports to improve your life. The new book will be excellent for diabetics, and for the maintenance phase as well.

Your feedback on this, my first book, would be appreciated. Any and all comments or questions are more than welcome. I hope I hear from you!

Blessings,

Sue Lillemo

Email: support@hcgrecipesbook.com

HCG Recipes website: http://hcgrecipesbook.com

Our business website: http://hcgmetamorphosis.com

Look for us on:
Facebook, Twitter, LinkedIn, and YouTube